EMPIRE OF THE ISLAMIC WORLD

REVISED EDITION

GREAT EMPIRES OF THE PAST

Empire of Alexander the Great

Empire of Ancient Egypt

Empire of Ancient Greece

Empire of Ancient Rome

Empire of the Aztecs

Empire of the Incas

Empire of the Islamic World

Empire of the Mongols

Empires of Ancient Mesopotamia

Empires of Ancient Persia

Empires of Medieval West Africa

Empires of the Maya

GREAT EMPIRES OF THE PAST

EMPIRE OF THE ISLAMIC WORLD

REVISED EDITION

ROBIN DOAK

STEPHEN CORY, HISTORICAL CONSULTANT

CHELSEA HOUSE
PUBLISHERS
An imprint of Infobase Publishing

Chelsea House
An imprint of Infobase Publishing
132 West 31st Street
New York NY 10001

Library of Congress Cataloging-in-Publication Data
Doak, Robin S. (Robin Santos), 1963–
  Empire of the Islamic world / Robin Doak. — Rev. ed.
      p. cm. — (Great empires of the past)
  Includes bibliographical references and index.
  ISBN 978-1-60413-161-1 (acid-free paper) 1. Islamic Empire--Juvenile literature. 2. Civilization, Islamic--Juvenile literature.
I. Title. II. Series.

  DS38.3.D63 2009
  909'.0976701--dc22

                              2009008934

Chelsea House books are available at special discounts when purchased in bulk quantities for businesses, associations, institutions, or sales promotions. Please call our Special Sales Department in New York at (212) 967-8800 or (800) 322-8755.

You can find Chelsea House on the World Wide Web at http://www.chelseahouse.com

Produced by the Shoreline Publishing Group LLC
Editorial Director: James Buckley Jr.
Series Editor: Beth Adelman
Text design by Annie O'Donnell
Cover design by Alicia Post
Composition by Mary Susan Ryan-Flynn
Cover printed by Bang Printing, Brainerd, MN
Book printed and bound by Bang Printing, Brainerd, MN
Date printed: November 2009

Printed in the United States of America

10 9 8 7 6 5 4 3 2 1

This book is printed on acid-free paper.

All links and Web addresses were checked and verified to be correct at the time of publication. Because of the dynamic nature of the Web, some addresses and links may have changed since publication and may no longer be valid.

CONTENTS

Introduction   7

PART I   HISTORY

CHAPTER 1   The Beginning of the Empire   17

CHAPTER 2   The Empire at Its Largest   35

CHAPTER 3   The Last Years of the Empire   45

PART II   SOCIETY AND CULTURE

CHAPTER 4   Society in the Islamic Empire   59

CHAPTER 5   Living in the Islamic Empire   73

CHAPTER 6   Islamic Art, Science, and Culture   95

Epilogue   121

Time Line   129

Glossary   131

Bibliography   133

Further Resources   135

Picture Credits   137

Index   138

About the Author   144

INTRODUCTION

FROM 632 TO 1258 THE ISLAMIC EMPIRE HAD THE MOST advanced culture and was the most powerful state in the world. Less than a century after it was founded, it had grown from a loose alliance of desert tribes into the largest empire in the history of the world. No ancient empire extended its reach farther around the globe. At its height, the Islamic Empire stretched from Spain in the west to the borders of India in the east, from central Asia in the north to North Africa in the south. The Muslim conquests led to the downfall of both the Persian and Byzantine Empires.

Throughout their newly conquered lands, the Muslims used the religion of Islam and the Arabic language to create a bond between the conquerors and the conquered. As a result, the Islamic Empire had religious, political, and cultural influences that survive to this day. Philip K. Hitti, a professor of Arab history, wrote in *The Arabs: A Short History*, "Islam is a way of life that has religious aspects, political aspects, and cultural aspects, and each of the three overlaps and interacts."

UNLIKELY BEGINNINGS

The Islamic Empire began in 632 in the hot, empty regions of the western Arabian Peninsula. This dry land was one-third desert, with few streams that flowed all year round. The empire had its roots in a religious movement, started by a man named Muhammad (ca. 570–632) who was born in Mecca, a city in modern-day Saudi Arabia. The laws of the empire were based on the messages Muhammad received from Allah (the Arabic word for God). People throughout the empire

CONNECTIONS

What Are Connections?

Throughout this book, and all the books in the Great Empires of the Past series, there are Connections boxes. They point out ideas, inventions, art, food, customs, and more from this empire that are still part of the world today. Nations and cultures in remote history can seem far away from the present day, but these connections demonstrate how our everyday lives have been shaped by the peoples of the past.

modeled their behavior on the moral teachings and the example set by Muhammad. Muslims believe that Muhammad lived the most perfect life ever.

The Islamic Empire was at its height during what is known in Western history as the early Middle Ages. The early Middle Ages date from around the collapse of the Roman Empire in the late sixth century, until the early 1100s. In Europe, ideas and culture did not advance much during this period. However, lands under the control of the Muslims were experiencing a golden age of learning, commerce, and civilization. Many ideas that came out of Islamic lands laid the foundation for a European rebirth of creativity and innovation in the 1400s, known as the Renaissance.

AGING KINGDOMS

By the early 400s, the once-mighty Roman Empire had broken into two empires, West and East. Although the Western Roman Empire did not last for long, the Eastern Roman Empire developed into a powerful entity known as the Byzantine Empire. The Byzantine Empire included the Balkan Peninsula and Asia Minor. The Byzantines also conquered much of the Middle East, including Egypt, as well as North Africa.

The Byzantines had competition for control of the Middle East. The Sassanian, or Persian, Empire dominated the areas to the southeast of Byzantium. The Sassanians ruled all of modern Iran and parts of what is today Iraq, Pakistan, Afghanistan, Turkmenistan, Uzbekistan, and the Gulf Coast of the Arabian Peninsula.

These two powerful empires were very different from one another, in both culture and religion. While the Byzantine Empire was a Christian kingdom, the Sassanians followed Zoroastrianism—a Persian religion founded by the prophet and teacher Zoroaster (ca. 630–ca. 553 B.C.E.).

The two empires were constantly at war with one another. Many important trade routes between the empires and their desirable goods ran through the Arabian Peninsula. Both the Byzantines and the Sassanians wanted control of these trade routes to China and the lands around the Indian Ocean. They therefore fought often for control of the Arabian Peninsula.

To pay for these wars, both empires placed heavy taxes on their citizens. These taxes, along with other restrictions, caused unrest in Sassanian and Byzantine lands, especially among the Arab tribes living on the edges of the two empires.

By the early 600s, the people in the region were ready for revolution. The constant warfare had left both empires weak and unable to keep a strong grip on the lands and peoples of the Middle East. And the Arabs themselves were ready for change.

THE ARABIAN PENINSULA BEFORE MUHAMMAD

In the early 600s, the Arabian Peninsula was a desert-like region with a few fertile areas on the edges. Towns were usually built around a spring or well of fresh water. But there were few of them, and they were spaced far apart. Most Arabs were Bedouin nomads who wandered from place to place in search of grazing land for their sheep. (Bedouin is an Arabic word that means "people of the desert.")

The Bedouins lived in tribes organized by family relationships. To become stronger, groups of tribes that were related by marriage or direct family ties might band together to form a larger, more powerful unit.

For the Bedouins, the most important thing was loyalty to one's tribe. Each tribe member depended upon the others to help them survive in the harsh desert environment. If one was killed by a member of another tribe, it was the duty of the injured person's tribe to take revenge. The principle of blood vengeance—killing the person who committed the injury—was a key part of tribal life.

Life in the desert was difficult. The world the Bedouins lived in was hot, dry, and often hostile. Camels were an important part of their lives, and a major means of transportation—earning the animals the nickname "ships of the desert."

Camels also provided support for the Bedouins. The camel's hair and hide was used to make tents and clothing. Camel manure was used as fuel, and its urine was used as a medicine, insect repellent, and shampoo. The Bedouins also ate camel meat to supplement their basic meal of dates and milk. According to historian Philip Hitti, the Arabic language may have as many as a thousand different words for the camel. The words describe camels of different breeds, conditions, and stages of growth.

Bedouins Today

Bedouins continue to make their homes in the deserts of the Arabian Peninsula and North Africa today. As many as 6 million people still live a nomadic life. The head of a tribe is known as the *sheikh*. Following ancient tradition, the position is given to the most senior male member of the tribe.

As in the past, the Bedouins rely heavily on the one-humped or dromedary camel. These hearty creatures store fat in their humps, and can go for up to six weeks with little food or water. They can also carry heavy loads and can walk as far as 100 miles in one day. These are important abilities to the nomadic Bedouins.

Bedouin camels are well-known for their speed. They can move at more than 10 miles per hour. In recent years, Bedouins have begun breeding camels in large numbers to sell to wealthy Arabs, who often use the camels for racing.

Bedouin tribes were almost always at war. In the harsh desert environment, where water—or the lack of it—could mean the difference between life and death, tribes often fought for control of the wells that dotted the region. Fertile grazing lands for camels and goats were also a source of conflict.

Raids on other tribes and towns on the desert borders were common. During these raids, the Bedouins took camels and other needed supplies. Any goods that were not obtained through raiding could later be purchased at the marketplaces in the few towns.

The Bedouin tribes looked down upon their neighbors who lived in the towns that dotted the western peninsula. For the townsfolk, life was easier and more settled. With the aid of reservoirs (natural or artificial lakes used to supply water) and irrigation (bringing water to the fields to help crops grow), some areas were able to support farming. Here, they grew barley, wheat, melons, dates, and nuts.

The business that proved the most important to the early towns, however, was trade. Regional trade routes ran through the western peninsula. Caravans (groups of people traveling together, often traders) of camels carried cloth, spices, and gemstones to port cities in Syria and Palestine. From these ports, the goods were then shipped to Yemen and around the eastern Mediterranean coast through the valley of the Tigris and Euphrates Rivers to the Persian Gulf.

The Arabs also produced some important products of their own. The ones most desired in other parts of the world were perfumes and incense, a substance burned for its sweet smell. The Arabs were especially known for producing frankincense and myrrh. These two scents were obtained from the gum of trees and shrubs. They were highly prized in the great empires of Rome, Egypt, Persia, and Babylon. They were also very valuable: In the New Testament of the Bible, the baby Jesus is given gifts of gold, frankincense, and myrrh by the Three Wise Men.

Before Muhammad was born, there were three major towns on the Arabian Peninsula. All were located in the Hijaz, a mountainous region on the western coast. Yathrib, the northernmost town, was made up of farms and small villages settled around an oasis (an area in the desert that has water and plants). Taif was a mountain resort area, used by wealthy Arabs to escape the summer heat.

Mecca, the third town, seemed to have the least potential for success. Mecca was located in a rocky area with few plants, and was surrounded by mountains. By the early 600s, however, it was the wealthiest and most important town on the peninsula.

Before the rise of Islam, two empires competed for control of the Middle East. The Byzantine Empire was part of the old Roman Empire. The Sassanian Empire was ruled by the Persians. This decorative item shows the Sassanian king Shapur I (r. ca. 239–ca. 272 C.E.) on the left fighting the Roman emperor Valerian (d. ca. 260 C.E.). Shapur won the battle.

MECCA

Mecca was the commercial center of the Arabian Peninsula. The town was an important stop along many caravan routes between Syria, Iraq, southwestern Arabia, and the Red Sea.

Mecca was also the center of religion for most Arabs. Before Muhammad, Arabian tribes practiced animism, a religion that believes objects in nature have souls or spirits. Stones, springs, or trees might be worshipped as sacred objects. The main god of the Arab people was Allah. Allah was believed to be the creator of the universe, and was much stronger than the other gods.

Mecca was at the heart of this animistic worship. Each year, thousands of pilgrims (people on a trip to a special sacred place) went to Mecca to take part in religious festivals. These festivals were centered around the Kaaba, a large cube-shaped building in the middle of town. The Kaaba was a one-room structure made of dark stone and covered with a black cloth. It was home to the sacred Black Stone. This stone, embedded in one of the walls, was believed to have been placed there originally by Adam, the first man, and later by the prophet Abraham. The Kaaba was also thought to be the home of the animistic god Hubal and more than 300 other minor gods.

This first-century B.C.E. container is shaped like a camel. It is made out of terra-cotta (a type of earthenware) and was found in Syria. Camels provided vital support for people who lived in the desert.

Although Mecca was a center of animistic worship, monotheism—the worship of one god—was also present. Groups of Jews and Christians lived throughout the region. The town of Yathrib, which would later play an important role in the spread of Islam, was home to a large Jewish population.

Mecca was controlled by a wealthy tribe of merchants called the Quraysh, who had become rich by controlling the entire town's trading business. They then took control of the government and appointed only members of their own tribe to positions on the town's council. As the ruling tribe, the Quraysh also controlled the care and maintenance of the Kaaba.

Around the year 610, a man from Mecca named Muhammad, who was also a member of the Quraysh, received a revelation from God. Muhammad began preaching about this revelation, and soon attracted a number of followers. The new religion was called Islam, and the followers of Muhammad the Prophet were called Muslims.

Over the years, many people were attracted to Muhammad and his message. This message included caring for poor people, living modestly, and following a strict moral code. The Islamic religion grew. When Muhammad died in 632, his followers began to spread the religion beyond the Arabian Peninsula.

Islam's founder was both a political and a religious leader. In the empire that grew up after him religion and politics were so tightly mixed that they could not be separated. The law of the empire was the law of Islam, which was given to Muhammad by God.

The leaders who came after Muhammad quickly conquered surrounding areas and tribes. They took control of lands on the Arabian Peninsula, and then stretched into the Byzantine and Sassanian Empires. In less than 100 years they held land on three continents and had created the largest empire the world had yet seen.

The conquerors generally did not force the people they conquered to adopt their religion or culture. However, many of the conquered people converted to Islam. Some converted to avoid paying a tax imposed on non-Muslims. Others converted out of a deep belief in the message of Muhammad. Because it was the language of the government, Arabic also spread. The Islamic Empire lasted for a little more than six centuries. Even after it fell, and Islam and Arabic continued to have an important effect on the world.

HOW THE EMPIRE AFFECTED HISTORY

Today modern connections to the ancient Islamic Empire can be found throughout the world: place names, words, cultural contributions, architecture, and medical, mathematical, and scientific innovations are just a few of the areas in which the empire has made lasting contributions. Although many of the contributions considered to be "Arab" were, in fact, borrowed from conquered peoples, the Muslims left their own unique mark on them.

The greatest and most lasting effect of the empire, however, is Islam. Although Islam is the world's youngest major religion, it currently has more followers than any other religion except Christianity. About 1.3 billion people around the globe are Muslims. It is also one of the fastest growing religions in the world.

Islam is a powerful political force in today's world. There are numerous countries in which Islam is the state religion (the religion officially endorsed by the state), including Iran, Iraq, Pakistan, and Afghanistan. There are also large Muslim populations in many other countries, including Indonesia, India, Israel, China, Russia, Bangladesh, and a number of nations in Central Asia. Although the Islamic religion was born on the Arabian Peninsula, most

CONNECTIONS

The Significance of Jinn

Many of the minor gods the Bedouins prayed to were forces of good. But there were also forces of mischief to be dealt with. And some spirits were both.

The jinn were spirits capable of taking the form of a human or an animal. They could also influence people for good or for bad. The Bedouins believed the jinn roamed the desert, causing trouble and spying on humans. However, some jinn also inspired poets.

According to the Quran (sometimes written as Koran), jinn were created out of smokeless fire. One of the best-known jinn is Satan, who was sent out from heaven by God because he refused to bow down to humans. The Quran states that after Muhammad began preaching, a group of jinn heard him and converted to Islam.

The singular of jinn is *jinni*, and in English this word is written as *genie.* The idea of genies was popularized in the West by the *Thousand and One Nights*, a collection of Arabian, Persian, and Indian folktales compiled over hundreds of years. The funny genie in the Disney Studios movie *Aladdin* is very different from the original jinn of the Bedouin world.

CONNECTIONS

Coffee

The history of coffee is something of a mystery. Most experts believe that coffee was first grown in Africa, probably in Ethiopia. Some historians believe coffee had made its way to the Arabian Peninsula by about 675. Others place its arrival there at around 1000. At the very latest, coffee was growing in Yemen by the 1400s.

Even the source of the word *coffee* is up for debate. Some say the drink takes its name from Kaffa, the Ethiopian province where coffee was first grown. Others say that it gets its name from an Arabic phrase once used to refer to wine, *al-qahwa*.

At first, coffee beans were chewed rather than ground, roasted, and turned into liquid. By the end of the 15th century, however, coffee had become a popular drink throughout the Middle East. Coffeehouses, where men could meet and socialize while enjoying a cup of the strong beverage, soon sprang up. According to Bernard Lewis in *The Middle East: A Brief History of the Last 2,000 Years*, the coffeehouse served as the Middle East's equivalent of the tavern in Europe. Philip

Hitti, in *History of the Arabs: From the Earliest Times to the Present*, calls coffee the "wine of Islam."

During the 16th century, the production and export of coffee from Yemen became an important part of Middle Eastern trade with Europe. Coffee quickly became as popular in Europe as it was in the Middle East. In the early 1640s, the first European coffeehouse opened for business in Venice, Italy.

Coffee may have been brought to the United States in 1607, when Captain John Smith helped found the first permanent British settlement in Jamestown, Virginia. After the Boston Tea Party in 1773, coffee became the drink of choice of American patriots seeking independence.

Today, coffee is still one of America's most popular beverages. In 2009, more than half of all American adults drank coffee every day, according to the National Coffee Association. Most coffee imported into the United States is a type called Arabian or Arabica coffee. However, most Arabian coffee today is grown in Central and South America.

Muslims today are not Arabs. Currently, between 15 percent and 20 percent of all Muslims are Arab.

In the United States, Muslims are an important minority. There are about 6 million Muslims in the United States. That number more than doubled from 1990. Large Muslim populations are found in Los Angeles, Detroit, and New York City. There are more than 1,200 mosques in the country, according to the Hartford Seminary, a multifaith educational institution in Hartford, Connecticut.

PART·1

HISTORY

THE BEGINNING OF THE EMPIRE

THE EMPIRE AT ITS LARGEST

THE LAST YEARS OF THE EMPIRE

وقال يا محمد ربّك يقرئك السلام ويخصّك بالمحبّة والاكرام

حقّ تعالى سنكا سلام فلدى ايتدى ايشته جبرائيل

سكا كوندرد وم كه سنوك امروكه مطيع اولا سنول

دوشمنلرو كى هلاك ايليه بننكيم كوكا كا ك ديبلر

CHAPTER 1

THE BEGINNING OF THE EMPIRE

THE SEEDS OF THE ISLAMIC EMPIRE WERE SOWN AROUND 570, when Muhammad ibn (son of) Abd Allah was born in Mecca. His father died before Muhammad was born. As was the custom, the small child was sent to a Bedouin family in the desert to be nursed, because Arabs believed that the desert provided a healthier environment for a child's growth than the city.

Muhammad (whose name means "worthy of praise" in Arabic) returned to Mecca when he was still very young. But tragedy followed him. His mother died when he was just six, and his grandfather died soon after. Muhammad was then raised by his father's brother, Abu Talib (d. 619). He was one of the most prominent of the wealthy Quraysh traders in Mecca and a chief of the Hashemite clan.

Despite his uncle's importance, Muhammad himself was a poor orphan—something he never forgot. Later, as leader of a powerful political and religious group, Muhammad was especially sympathetic to the poor, orphaned, and disadvantaged.

Like most young men of his time, Muhammad learned archery (shooting with a bow and arrow), horsemanship, swordplay, and the principles of trading. Under his uncle's guidance, he began leading trade caravans across the desert. He soon earned a reputation as a competent and honest businessman. Before long, people were calling him al-Amin, which means "the trustworthy."

When Muhammad was 25 years old, he married Khadija (d. 620), the wealthy widow of a Mecca merchant. She was 15 years older than he. The two met when Muhammad began leading trading caravans

OPPOSITE
This scene is from a ca. 1595 book made in Turkey about the life of Muhammad. It shows the prophet with his father-in-law, Abu Bakr, and his son-in-law, Ali. Muhammad is shown with veiled face because Islam discourages the depiction of people, especially Muhammad.

for Khadija. Muhammad is said to have loved his wife, and their relationship was a strong one: Although polygamy (the practice of having more than one wife) was common among Arab men, Muhammad took no other wives for the 25 years he was married to Khadija. Together, the couple had at least six children, although Muhammad's two sons died when they were just infants. Of his four daughters, Fatima (ca. 605–633), the oldest, was his favorite.

Even before he received his revelation from God, Muhammad displayed wisdom and diplomatic skills. When he was in his mid 30s, the Kaaba was damaged in a flood. As the leading tribe in Mecca, the Quraysh were put in charge of rebuilding it. After the work was done, however, the chief members of the tribe's different segments began arguing about who should have the privilege of placing the Black Stone back in its home. Muhammad solved the problem by having one man from each of the four groups who had worked on the Kaaba carry the stone together on a cloth. Muhammad himself placed the stone into the corner wall.

As he got older, Muhammad sought peace and time alone in a cave in the cliffs of Hira, a nearby mountain. Here he would meditate (think deeply with the mind focused on just one thing), and eventually begin to see visions and hear someone speaking to him.

In 610, Muhammad received a visit from the angel Gabriel, who was sent to him by God. Gabriel instructed him to make *quran*—which means "to recite" in Arabic. Gabriel meant Muhammad should recite the word of God.

Terrified and confused, Muhammad fled for home. But on the way, Gabriel confronted him again, saying, "O Muhammad, you are the apostle of God." (An apostle is a messenger or representative.) At first Muhammad thought he might be losing his sanity. The angelic visits stopped. But a year later, he received another message. Muhammad then embraced his role as God's prophet and opened himself up to the messages. Over the next 20 years he continued to receive revelations from God.

Three years after receiving his first message Muhammad began preaching what had been revealed to him. After his death these revelations were collected into a book called the Quran. This holy scripture of Islam provided the laws and regulations for the new community gathering around Muhammad's teachings.

CONNECTIONS

The Kaaba Today

The Kaaba has been rebuilt many times throughout the centuries. Today it is a cube-shaped building about 50 feet tall, enclosed by the Grand Mosque of Mecca. Two of the Kaaba's walls measure about 40 feet long, while the other two walls are about 35 feet long. The area around the Kaaba can hold hundreds of thousands of worshippers at one time. One of the most recent additions is a solid gold gate.

The black silk cloth that covers the Kaaba is decorated with black calligraphy (fancy writing) patterns. Passages from the Quran are embroidered on the cloth with gold thread. Each year, a new cloth is made to be draped over the Kaaba.

The Black Stone is embedded in the southeast corner of the Kaaba. Muslims believe this stone was placed there by Adam. The stone, which may be a meteorite, measures 11 inches wide and 15 inches high. Over the years, the stone has broken into several pieces and it is now surrounded by a silver frame to hold it together. In the corner opposite the Black Stone lies a reddish stone, called the Stone of Felicity.

The Kaaba is the focus point of all Muslim prayers to Mecca. Within the Kaaba, people can face in any direction when they pray. Outside the Kaaba, all Muslims face it to pray—no matter where they are in the world. A 12-mile area around the Kaaba is declared *haram*, or restricted. Only Mus-

Modern pilgrims walk around the Kaaba during the final day of the hajj. The Kaaba is at the heart of the Grand Mosque in Mecca, Saudi Arabia.

lims are allowed to enter this area, and, as a sacred site, the spilling of blood and other unreligious actions are prohibited.

Each year, more than 2 million Muslims travel to the Kaaba during the pilgrimage season (the last month of the Islamic year). It is the end point of the hajj (pilgrimage) that all Muslims who can afford it are required to make at least once in their lives. In addition, thousands more make *umra*—a trip to the Kaaba at other times of the year. The pilgrims circle the Kaaba and kiss the Black Stone. It is important to remember, however, that the Black Stone itself is not an object of worship. Pilgrims are simply following the tradition set by Muhammad himself.

IN THEIR OWN WORDS

The Life of Muhammad

This biography of Muhammad was written by Ibn Ishaq (ca. 704–773). It is one of the few full biographies of the prophet. In this section, Muhammad is relating something mystical that happened to him—an encounter with beings who washed the last drop of blackness from his heart.

[W]hile I was with a brother of mine behind our tents shepherding the lambs, two men in white raiment [clothing] came to me with a gold basin full of snow. Then they seized me and opened up my belly, extracted my heart and split it; then they extracted a black drop from it and threw it away; then they washed my heart and my belly with that snow until they had thoroughly cleansed them. Then one said to the other, "Weigh him against ten of his people"; they did so and I outweighed them. Then they weighed me against a hundred and then a thousand, and I outweighed them. He said, "Leave him alone, for by God, if you weighed him against all his people he would outweigh them." . . .

(Source: Ibn Ishaq. "Selections from the Life of Muhammad." Medieval Sourcebook. Available online. URL: http://www.fordham. edu/halsall/source/muhammadi-sira.html. Accessed March 6, 2008.)

Muhammad preached that there was only one God, Allah, and that all must submit to his will and worship only him. Muhammad's new religion eventually became known as Islam, which is the Arabic word for submission. His followers were called Muslims, or "those who submit." The Quran also laid out rules for everyday life. These included prayer schedules, marriage and divorce laws, and rules for the treatment of slaves, prisoners of war, enemies, and orphans.

At first Muhammad's followers consisted only of his close family and a few friends. Slowly, however, the little group grew. Because the teachings of the Quran included the equality of all people and charity to the poor, it was very attractive to the underprivileged of Mecca. The new religion also gave followers the hope of an afterlife, where they would be judged for their worldly deeds. Those who lived by God's word would go to heaven, while those who had sinned would spend eternity in hell.

Muhammad attacked idol worship (worshipping images of a god), which was an important money-making industry for Mecca. This angered the wealthy merchants. So did his messages of equality and the duty to care for the underprivileged. Not only was Muhammad threatening the importance of the Quraysh, but he was attacking ancient tribal ways of life by preaching that God should be placed before tribal ties.

The Quraysh began harassing him and his followers. Muslims were at first greeted with jeers and ridicule. When this failed to convince them to turn away from their faith, the attacks on Muhammad and his followers turned violent. In one case, a slave who had converted to Islam was placed in the burning desert sun with stones on his chest and left to die. One of Muhammad's stepsons was stoned and killed while praying at the Kaaba. Small armed battles between Muslims and the Quraysh became common. To escape the violence, some of Muhammad's followers fled from Mecca to Ethiopia, in northeastern Africa.

In a final attempt to quiet Muhammad and diminish his influence, the Quraysh refused to allow him to worship at the Kaaba. Then Muhammad's uncle died in 619, and other members of his tribe withdrew their protection from him. These events placed Muhammad in serious danger.

He began searching for a town that would welcome him and his followers. He first turned to Taif, a thriving farming town south of Mecca. Because some members of Muhammad's tribe lived there, he expected a welcome. But instead, they drove Muhammad from town.

Muhammad finally found a home in the town of Yathrib, where a number of Muslim converts already lived. The people welcomed him as a mediator (someone who helps resolve disagreements) and problem-solver. In 622, his followers began the journey to Yathrib. Muhammad, along with his friend and father-in-law, Abu Bakr (573–634), was one of the last to leave. Learning of a plot to kill Muhammad, the two men fled from Mecca in the dead of night.

The journey to Yathrib is known as the Hijra, or "migration," and is an important event in Islamic history. The Hijra is considered the official birth of the Islamic religion. It is also considered the birth of the *umma*, the Muslim community, and the beginning of the Muslim calendar.

Yathrib was eventually renamed Medina, from the Arabic *madinat al-nabi*, or "City of the Prophet." Muhammad's time in Medina is called the Medinan period. The *umma*—a community based on a shared religion, not on kinship and blood ties—flowered during this period.

During his 10 years in Medina, Muhammad became more than just a spiritual leader. He put his administrative and political skills to good

The Basics of Islam

Before Islam the Arabs worshipped a number of gods and idols. They also worshipped stones, trees, and wells—a belief called *animism*. However, the Arabs still recognized a main god, whom they called Allah.

Islam appeared centuries after Judaism and Christianity. Muhammad admired the Bible, and many stories from the Old Testament are mentioned in the Quran. So is Jesus. Muslims recognize a number of Biblical figures as the prophets of God, including Adam, Abraham, Moses, and Jesus. As God's messengers, they are all respected and honored by Muslims. So is Mary, Jesus' mother. However, Jesus is not recognized as a god.

Muslims do not believe Muhammad was a god, either. Rather, he was God's final prophet—a carrier of God's divine message and the living example of how to lead a religious and good life. The Islamic religion believes that there is only one God, and that is Allah.

The Five Pillars of Islam, or Arkan al-Islam, are the five fundamental actions that should be performed by all Muslims, no matter what branch of Islam they follow. They are:

1. Declaration of belief: That is, belief in one God, Allah. To do this, Muslims repeat a phrase known as the *shahada*:
"There is no God but Allah and Muhammad is His Prophet."
2. Prayer: Muslims pray five times a day, at fixed times. These daily prayers are known together as *salat*.
3. Charity: During the early days of the empire, the Muslims developed two types of tithes, or religious taxes: a voluntary tithe, or *sadaqa*, and a required tithe, or *zakat*. The *zakat* was used to provide for widows, orphans, and the poor. It could also be used to ransom captives, help slaves buy their freedom, and equip volunteers for jihad. Today, the *zakat* is 2.5 percent of one's assets and income-generating properties. Shiites also pay an additional tithe of 20 percent on all new income.
4. Fasting: During the month of Ramadan (the ninth month of the Islamic calendar), Muslims must not have food, drink, or sexual relations from dawn to sunset each day. This fasting is known as *saum*.
5. Pilgrimage: All Muslims who can afford it should make a journey to Mecca at least once in their lifetime during the hajj, or time of pilgrimage. The hajj occurs during the first 10 days of Dhu al-Hijja (the 12th month of the Islamic calendar.)

use, effectively acting as the town's leader. All of the legal and political decisions in Medina reflected the words of God as revealed through Muhammad. Muhammad's power also improved the lives of Muslims in the town. While they had been persecuted in Mecca, in Medina they had prestige and influence. Islam was evolving from a religious movement to a powerful political one.

FIRST BATTLES

To help support his new community, Muhammad and the Muslims soon began raiding trading caravans making their way to and from Mecca. The Muslims practiced the Arab custom of the raid, or *razzia*. In the book *Muhammad: Prophet and Statesman*, W. Montgomery Watt says the raid was "a normal feature of Arab desert life. It was a kind of sport rather than war."

The attackers would surprise their victims, take what they wanted, then disappear again. Hand-to-hand combat was rare. During the raids, the Muslims took both goods and hostages. These raids greatly disrupted Mecca's economy.

Muhammad said he had received a message from God concerning the rightness of these actions. The Quran (chapter 22, verse 39) states, "Permission to take up arms is hereby given to those who are attacked, because they have been wronged." Because Muhammad and his followers had been attacked in Mecca, they believed the raids were justified as a way of fighting back.

The Quraysh were, of course, alarmed by the raids. They believed that when Muhammad left Mecca,

In the Battle of Badr, Muhammad and his followers defeated the Quraysh of Mecca. This scene from the battle is an illustration from a book about Muhammad's life that was made in 1594–1595 in Turkey.

they had seen the last of him. They lived on the profits of their trade, and they would not tolerate its disruption.

In 624 Muhammad led about 315 Muslims from Medina to Badr, a stopover for trade caravans located 90 miles south of Medina. They waited to ambush a large caravan they knew would be passing through. However, word of the ambush got back to Mecca. The Quraysh were determined to wipe out the troublesome Muslims, and sent nearly 1,000 men to punish Muhammad and his followers.

The Battle of Badr began with several warriors from each side challenging one another to single combat. This was an ancient Arab custom. After the single combat, the Muslim troops raced into battle, shouting the battle cry "Allahu Akbar!" ("God is most great!"). The men fought hard using swords and arrows. Although the Muslims were outnumbered three to one and were poorly armed and lacked experience, they were disciplined and unafraid to die. Before the battle Muhammad promised his warriors that anyone who died fighting for Islam that day would immediately enter paradise. To the surprise of many, the Muslims won the victory. Afterwards Muhammad would not allow his men to slaughter the enemy captives, as was the custom of the time.

Muhammad's victory was seen by his followers as a sign from God that the Muslim raids were just and right. One of Allah's messages to Muhammad, as recorded in the Quran (chapter 21, verse 105), was, "The righteous among My servants shall inherit the earth." After the Battle of Badr, Bedouin tribes flocked to Medina to offer their allegiance to Muhammad. The Bedouins were known as fierce fighters, on horseback and on foot, and their presence attracted even more tribes, who journeyed to Medina to offer their support or pledge peace.

After the Battle of Badr, tensions between Muhammad and the Jews of Medina came to a head. Some of this tension was political and some was religious. The Jews did not recognize Muhammad's claim to be a prophet in the line of the ancient Jewish prophets. And the Muslims accused them of supporting the Meccans. One of Medina's Jewish tribes was forced to leave the town, and the Muslims took over the property of everyone who fled. Later, a second Jewish tribe was expelled. Finally, in 627, Muhammad accused the remaining Jews of cooperating with the enemy Meccans. About 600 Jewish men were beheaded, and the women and children were sold into slavery.

After their humiliating defeat at Badr, the Meccans prepared to try again to defeat Muhammad. In 625, they sent 3,000 men to attack

Idols and Islamic Art

When Muhammad destroyed the idols in Mecca, he set in motion an artistic style that continues to this day. Art showing human beings is prohibited in mosques and on materials used for worship. Islamic art generally uses geometric shapes and calligraphy (decorative writing) rather than representational forms.

the Muslims outside Medina. At the Battle of Uhud, Muhammad himself was wounded and the Muslims were overpowered and forced to retreat. However, the Meccans were not able to capture Medina itself.

Over the next three years, dozens of battles took place between the Meccans and the Muslims in Medina. Muhammad himself led about 20 of these battles. Finally, in 628, Muhammad negotiated a truce (an agreement to stop fighting) with the Meccans and in the following year returned as a pilgrim to the city's holy sites. However, the murder of one of his followers provoked him to attack the city, which soon surrendered.

Muhammad acted generously to the Meccans, demanding only that the idols around the Kaaba be destroyed. "Truth has come and falsehood has vanished," he said. Muhammad declared that the area around the Kaaba was now a sanctuary, a holy place to the One God, Allah. Mecca was a Muslim city.

Muhammad was not harsh with the Meccans. He awarded the Quraysh positions of authority and power. It was a very smart move. Soon the Quraysh were helping Muhammad abolish the worship of idols and subdue area tribes. The Muslims sent troops out to the surrounding areas to destroy animistic temples. With that kind of persuasion, the number of converts to Islam grew rapidly.

This is a page from a mid-16th century book that contained instructions for pilgrims on the hajj.

MUHAMMAD'S SUCCESSORS

In early 632, Muhammad made another journey from Medina to Mecca. On this pilgrimage, called the hajj, Muhammad was accompanied by 30,000 of his followers. During the hajj, pilgrims had to follow

CONNECTIONS

Facing Mecca

Today, Muslims around the world turn their faces toward Mecca when they pray. In every mosque, one can find a mihrab, or niche, that indicates in which direction the faithful should pray. Above many mihrabs are the words Muhammad received in revelation (as recorded in the Quran): "Many a time have we seen you turn your face toward the sky. We will make you turn toward a *qibla* [direction] that will please you. Turn your face toward the Holy Mosque [the Kaaba in Mecca]; wherever you be, turn your faces toward it."

strict rules of behavior. There was to be no violence, no sexual intercourse, no arguing or ill will.

When he arrived in Mecca, Muhammad began a ritual that modern-day pilgrims continue to follow. He circled the Kaaba seven times. Then he kissed and touched the Black Stone. Other parts of Muhammad's ritual included going back and forth between two hills seven times, throwing pebbles at three pillars representing Satan, and slaughtering sheep to commemorate Abraham's willingness to sacrifice his son Ishmael to God. (In the Jewish and Christian bibles, it is Isaac whom God asks Abraham to sacrifice; Muslims disagree with this version of events.)

This first hajj, often called the Farewell Pilgrimage, was Muhammad's last trip to Mecca. He seemed to know that his life was coming to an end. Preaching a sermon on the plain of Arafat, Muhammad told his followers, "I do not know whether I shall ever meet you in this place again."

A few months after returning to Medina, Muhammad became ill and died. At the time of his death, he was the most powerful political and religious leader in the region. In just 20 years, he had conquered or won over most of the tribes on the Arabian Peninsula. He had destroyed animism and idol worship, replacing these practices with a strong new monotheistic religion. Perhaps most important, he had started a new way of life for the community of Muslims.

Muhammad's followers believed he was so close to God that at first, many thought it impossible that he was dead. Some said he would return. Abu Bakr, Muhammad's father-in-law and companion, finally spoke to the grieving Muslims. "If you worshipped Muhammad, know that he is dead," he said. "But if you worship the One God, know that he is alive and does not die."

After Muhammad died, a serious question arose that had the potential to create a crisis for the young religion: Should there be one leader or many to replace Muhammad as the religious and political leader of the *umma*? And who, exactly, should take the great prophet's place as leader of the Muslims and the Arab people? Muhammad had been the absolute ruler of the Islamic community, but he had not named a successor.

Two groups emerged with very different opinions on the matter. One group believed Muhammad had selected his son-in-law and cousin, Ali (d. 661), to be the caliph, or successor, after his death. Ali was married to Muhammad's favorite daughter, Fatima, and was one of the first to have accepted Islam. The group who believed in Ali's claim became known as the Shia, or "party of" Ali, also known as Shiites.

The second—and larger—group did not believe Muhammad had named any particular person to be his successor. They chose to follow Arab tribal custom and allow the senior men of the *umma* to choose the next ruler. The men decided Muhammad's successor should be selected from a group of his oldest and most faithful companions. After much discussion, they chose Abu Bakr. Those who supported Abu Bakr became known as the people of the sunna (the traditions and examples of the prophet), or Sunnis. Today, about 88 percent of all Muslims are Sunni, while 11 percent are Shiite.

There was much controversy, but Abu Bakr became the first caliph. He was the first of four of Muhammad's companions who would eventually rule the early Islamic Empire. These first four leaders are known collectively as the "rightly guided" caliphs.

The first four caliphs were the most connected to the *umma*. They were in charge of the political and religious life of the Muslim community, and they directed the raids and wars that led to the expansion of the empire. Although all four had been companions of Muhammad, none reigned without problems or dissent. Only Abu Bakr died a natural death. The last three were murdered.

CONQUEST BEGINS

Abu Bakr chose Medina as his capital. He was a wise and religious man, and he had the support of the people of Mecca and Medina, as well as some of the area tribes. Still other tribes, however, broke away from Islam when Muhammad died. Many felt that they had pledged their loyalty and obedience to Muhammad the leader, not to Islam the religion.

Abu Bakr moved swiftly to conquer those tribes that tried to pull away. He placed Khalid ibn al-Walid (d. 642), known as the Sword of Islam, in charge of the fighting. Khalid was a great military leader and was brilliant at planning strategy. Historian Philip Hitti, in *The Arabs: A Short History*, calls his campaigns "among the most brilliantly executed in the history of warfare."

The Muslim troops were made up of volunteers from various tribes, and Khalid's first task was molding them into a unified fighting machine. The army was divided into divisions, each with an assigned place on the battlefield, including a center, two wings, a vanguard (in the front), and a rear guard. Tribesmen fought together within these divisions. Each tribe had its own banner, which was carried into battle attached to a lance (a weapon with a hard point mounted on a wooden pole).

The general excelled in surprise attacks. With lightning speed, he would ride out of the desert on horseback, his cavalry behind him on horses and camels. He trained his cavalry to use the lance, and it soon became one of the most feared weapons in the world when carried by a Muslim soldier.

Backing up the cavalry was the infantry—soldiers on foot. They were armed with bows and arrows, slingshots, and swords. To protect themselves, the Muslim soldiers wore a light coat of mail (interlocking metal links) and carried a shield.

The battles to bring the rebellious tribes under control are known as the Ridda wars. *Ridda* is an Arabic word that means "leaving the religion." As the tribes were conquered, they once again gave their loyalty to Islam and the new caliph. As a result, the number of troops fighting for Islam swelled. This marked the beginning of the first Islamic army.

By the time he died in 634, Abu Bakr had united the entire Arabian Peninsula under the

CONNECTIONS

The Arabian Horse

Most horse lovers are familiar with a beautiful breed of horse known as the Arabian. The Arabian descended from horses that came to the Arabian Peninsula from North Africa and Mesopotamia (modern-day Iraq). It was probably the first domesticated breed of horse in the world. These animals were valued by wealthy Bedouins for their speed, beauty, and strength.

In the eighth century, the Arabian horse was brought to Spain during the Islamic conquest of that region. Eventually, it was bred with English horses. Several breeds that are very common now have the Arabian horse as part of their heritage. These breeds include the Thoroughbred, American Saddle Horse, and Quarter Horse.

banner of Islam. He had also begun raiding parts of Syria and Iraq—regions controlled by the Byzantine and Sassanian Empires.

Before his death, Abu Bakr picked Umar ibn al-Khattab (ca. 581–644) as his successor, the second "rightly guided" caliph. Umar, like Abu Bakr, had been one of Muhammad's closest companions. Umar was the first caliph to use the title Commander of the Faithful. All future caliphs would also claim this title.

Umar was tall and energetic, intelligent and just. He chose a simple lifestyle even when the riches of conquered kingdoms were in his hands. He ruled for 10 years, gaining a reputation as a man of wisdom and honor. He was responsible for introducing Islamic law and administrative functions to the conquered territories. He was especially noted for carefully following the laws of Islam. He even had his own son whipped to death for drunkenness and immoral behavior.

Under Umar's command, Islamic troops continued their advance into neighboring regions controlled by the Byzantine and Sassanian Empires. These advances were a result of a strategy that was agreed upon in advance by the caliph, his officials, and the commanders of the armies of Medina, Mecca, and Taif.

From Medina, Umar sent troops to what is now the central Middle East. Before long, the Byzantine regions of Syria, Palestine, and Egypt were all in Muslim hands. Although the Byzantine ruler sent forces to oppose the invading troops, the Muslims had a huge advantage: knowledge of the desert. Arabian troops knew how to survive in the harsh environment. Their opponents did not. Safe in the dry, hostile land, the Islamic generals ordered their troops to wait until the enemy believed the threat of attack had passed. Then the Muslims would fly from the desert, attack, and conquer.

Khalid was a master of desert warfare. In early 635, Umar ordered his greatest general to make a 200-mile march across the desert to attack Damascus, the capital of Syria and a stronghold of the Byzantine Empire. According to legend, Khalid took camels that had gorged themselves with water. From time to time, the general ordered some of these camels to be killed so that the horses could drink the water stored in their humps and the men could eat their meat. After a six-month siege, Khalid and his men eventually took control of Damascus. (A siege is a type of warfare in which a town or fort is cut off from the outside so it cannot receive supplies and the citizens cannot escape. Eventually they run out of food and must surrender.)

Commander of the Faithful

Today, Morocco's King Mohammed VI (b. 1963) claims the title Commander of the Faithful. King Mohammed, the religious and political leader of the North African country, claims to be a direct descendant of the prophet Muhammad. The kings of Morocco have claimed this title since the 16th century, although it is not recognized by Muslims outside of Morocco.

Another person who claims the title of Commander of the Faithful is Mohammad Omar, Supreme Leader of the Taliban, the political party that controlled most of Afghanistan from 1996 to 2001. Omar took the title of Commander of the Faithful in 1996, but was not recognized as such by Muslims outside Afghanistan.

Under Siege

Siege warfare, although new to the Muslims, was an important battle strategy in the Middle Ages. During a siege, attackers prevent supplies and people from entering or exiting the city. The attackers might also use giant logs called battering rams and other weapons to weaken the city's walls. Sieges could drag on for months—essentially starving the citizens of the town into surrender.

Following Muhammad's example, Khalid was not cruel to the people he conquered. Before entering Damascus, the general promised the city's residents that they would be safe and that their city would not be destroyed. Khalid also promised that Muslim soldiers would not stay in their homes. He guaranteed that, as long as the people of Damascus paid the tax required by the caliph, they had nothing to fear.

As the Muslim troops advanced through the rest of the Byzantine Empire, they met with little resistance. In many cases, the conquered people welcomed the invaders with open arms and even cooperated with the Muslim attackers. Many were unhappy with the harsh Byzantine rule. There is evidence that even some Christian groups that followed different beliefs from mainstream Christianity were persecuted by the Byzantines. Other towns surrendered rather than face the fierce Arab fighters they had heard about.

These conquests were known as *jihad*, or "holy wars." Many Muslims saw the battles as efforts to fight evil and spread the message of Muhammad and the idea of monotheism. Those who died on the battlefield were considered to be martyrs who won a place in heaven by their death on behalf of Islam.

There were other, more material reasons for the conquests, as well. The Arabian Peninsula was a desert with little plant life or water. The inhabitants needed food and supplies. They found plentiful supplies in the lands they conquered. These regions were some of the most fertile areas in the world.

But Muslim soldiers also found much more. The Arabian tribes were used to a simple, hard desert life, and were astonished by the wealth and riches of the cities they conquered. Being a soldier for the Islamic Empire became a much desired profession because it paid very well. Arabs who survived the almost constant battles and attacks got rich. Those who were killed while fighting to spread Islam earned a place in paradise.

At the same time they were conquering the Byzantine regions, Muslim armies were also chipping away at the Sassanian Empire. To defeat that weakened empire, Umar chose Saad ibn Abi Waqqas (d. 674) to lead the jihad. Saad was well-known to all Muslims. A close companion of Muhammad, he was said to have shed the first blood in defense of Islam back in Mecca before the Hijra. A seasoned warrior at the age of 40, Saad had also fought by Muhammad's side at the Battle of Badr. As a result, Muhammad had promised Saad that he, along with nine others, was assured a place in paradise.

In 637, Saad and his troops made their camp across the Euphrates River near Kadisiya in southern Iraq. The general sent representatives to the court of the Sassanian king. He turned them away and ordered his troops to cross the Euphrates River and attack the Muslims. Before the battle, the Muslim soldiers recited parts of the Quran. Then a number of soldiers from both sides engaged in single combat.

The Sassanians were a very different enemy than any the Muslims had faced before. The Sassanians had 33 Asian elephants carrying on their backs *howdahs* (carts) filled with soldiers. From here, the soldiers could safely throw spears at their Muslim opponents.

The battle raged until nightfall, when both sides retreated for the night. That evening, the Muslim troops danced and recited poetry—ancient tales of Arab bravery and victories. The following day, the battle resumed. This time, the Muslims had reinforcements and the Sassanians had left their elephants at home. To frighten the Sassanians' horses, the Muslims rode camels covered with hoods and other cloths. After the second day of fighting, however, neither side could claim victory.

After battling a third day without any clear winner, some of the Bedouin tribes decided to take matters into their own hands. That evening, they launched an attack on the Sassanian army that came to be called the Night of Fury. Fighting continued into dawn, until some Muslim soldiers broke through Sassanian lines and killed their general. The remaining Sassanian troops fled. Many died while trying to escape, either killed by Muslim soldiers or drowned while trying to cross the Euphrates River.

The hard-fought victory left the Sassanian Empire with few defenses. Saad and his troops soon conquered the old empire's capital, Ctesiphon (20 miles southeast of modern Baghdad in Iraq). Here, the general moved into the former king's royal palace and made part of it into a mosque. He also took the rest of the king's and his followers' property.

By the mid 650s, the Muslims had conquered a vast area that included the whole Arabian Peninsula, parts of North Africa, large pieces of the Byzantine Empire, and most of the Sassanian Empire. They had even reached the borders of India. From their new lands, the troops continued their assault into the surrounding regions, pushing onward in their quest for more land and riches.

And they found plenty of riches, especially in such cities as Damascus, Alexandria, and Ctesiphon. The Arabs were used to a simple way of life with very few possessions. They were amazed by the luxurious royal palaces and the wide variety of exotic goods they seized. One precious item, previously unknown to many of the Muslim invaders, was gold. Some soldiers even traded their share of gold for silver because they did not realize that gold was so valuable.

One conquest that was especially important to the Muslims was the capture of Jerusalem from the Byzantine Empire in 637. All three of the major monotheistic religions regard Jerusalem as a holy city. For Jews, it is the city of David (d. ca. 970 B.C.E.) and Solomon (ca. 974–ca. 922 B.C.E.), Israel's two greatest kings, and the site of the original Temple. For Christians, it is the place of Jesus' crucifixion, his tomb, and his resurrection. Muslims believe Muhammad was transported to heaven from Jerusalem to hear the word of God before being returned to Mecca. After Mecca and Medina, Jerusalem is the third holiest city for Muslims. The Muslims controlled Jerusalem for most of the next 1,300 years.

TROUBLE WITHIN

Umar was killed in 644 by a Persian Christian slave. He was stabbed with a poisoned dagger as he said morning prayers in the mosque. Uthman ibn Affan (ca. 574–656), a member of Mecca's important Quraysh family and Muhammad's son-in-law, was chosen to replace him as the third rightly guided caliph. During his 12 years as caliph, Uthman continued the conquests that the two caliphs before him had begun. The Islamic Empire extended north as far as the Caucasus Mountains in southeastern Europe. He pushed farther into North Africa and finished off the Sassanian Empire to the east.

Uthman, known as "the unpopular," was the first caliph who did not enjoy the widespread support of the Muslim community. Soon after taking power, the riches and wealth from the conquests began to fall off and he began to lose popularity among the Muslim soldiers. He lost even more support when he awarded conquered lands to members of his own family and those of his favorites. Uthman angered other Muslims by appointing members of his family to important positions, taking money from the conquests, and acting in ways that many felt were not fitting for the leader of the *umma*.

Armed revolts soon sprang up against the caliph. In 656, Uthman was murdered by a group of angry Muslim soldiers while he was reading the Quran. This was the first time a caliph had been killed by other Muslims.

The murder of Uthman sparked the First Civil War, which lasted from 656 to 661. During the war (known in Arabic as *fitna*, which means "time of trial"), the most important Muslim families struggled for control of the growing empire. One of those groups supported Ali, Muhammad's cousin and son-in-law. Ali had a close blood link to Muhammad—closer even than the first three caliphs. He had also been one of the original converts to Islam and had the support of most of the people of Medina and others in his party. They believed he should have been the first caliph and that the time had come to give him the title he deserved.

However, many people—especially the Umayyad family, Uthman's relatives—held Ali responsible for the third caliph's murder and did not think him worthy of being the caliph. The leader of the Umayyad opposition was Muawiya (602–680), governor of Damascus and a relative of the slain Uthman. Other prominent opponents included two early followers of Muhammad, and Muhammad's favorite wife in later years, Aisha (613–678).

Ali's opponents came to blows with Muawiya near Basra in southern Iraq. Here they were defeated at the Battle of the Camel in 656. During the battle, Aisha sat on the back of a camel in the midst of the fighting, urging her army to victory. The Battle of the Camel marked the first time Muslims fought against one another. It would not be the last.

Ali won the victory and became the fourth caliph. He moved the capital of the empire from Medina to Kufa, a fortified town in Iraq. In 657, Ali and his troops traveled north to Syria to attack Muawiya. But after a few small battles, Ali and Muawiya decided the conflict should be resolved through negotiations.

Some of Ali's Shiite supporters did not agree. Their battle cry, "Only God has the right to decide," reflected their belief that right or wrong must be decided on the battlefield. They believed that God would support those who deserved victory. This group of Shiites left Ali in Kufa. They became known as the Kharijites, or seceders. The Kharijites believed that only those who did not sin could truly be Muslims. This belief led them to oppose many later caliphs.

Ali was furious at the betrayal of the Kharijites and chased them to eastern Iraq, where his troops massacred many of them. His revenge against his former supporters further reduced his support among many Muslims.

Ali ruled for five stormy, war-torn years. Throughout his time as caliph, problems within the Muslim community grew and deepened. In 661, Ali was murdered in the Kufa mosque when a Kharijite assassin stabbed him with a poisoned dagger. His death marked a split among Muslims throughout the empire.

CHAPTER 2

THE EMPIRE AT ITS LARGEST

IN 660 (A YEAR BEFORE THE DEATH OF ALI, THE FOURTH rightly guided caliph), Muawiya had himself proclaimed caliph in Jerusalem. A year later, when Ali was killed, Muawiya took complete control of the empire. He became the first ruler of the Umayyad dynasty—named for the Umayyad family. Muawiya's father had led the opposition to Muhammad in Mecca many years before. However, he later converted to Islam, and the intelligent and literate Muawiya had served as Muhammad's secretary.

Muawiya ruled the Islamic Empire capably for 20 years. He maintained a strong, stable government and was actively involved in the business of governing his huge empire. He oversaw taxation, the army, and new conquests. He also was the first caliph to make Muslim coins for the empire, both gold and silver.

An important part of Muawiya's success was his selection of strong governors to control conquered lands throughout the empire. He chose capable men, often from his own family or tribe, to be the chief administrators of the various regions.

The new caliph was also a clever diplomat. His motto was, "I apply not my sword when my lash [whip] suffices, nor my lash when my tongue is enough," (quoted in Philip K. Hitti's *The Arabs: A Short History*). He meant that he did not use a lot of force when a little was enough to get things done. Muawiya was not against using force when necessary, however. The caliph knew that the best way to keep restless soldiers from becoming rebellious was to keep them busy conquering new lands. Under his reign, the empire expanded dramatically.

OPPOSITE

The Umayyad Mosque in Damascus, Syria, is one of the largest and oldest mosques in the world. The tomb of Saladin, a famous Islamic military leader, stands in a small garden next to the north wall of the mosque. In addition, the mosque holds a shrine that is said to contain the head of John the Baptist, who is honored as a prophet by both Christians and Muslims.

CONNECTIONS

Silk and Steel

During the Umayyad dynasty, the capital city of Damascus was an important trade center. The capital was famous for damask, a type of silk cloth embroidered with intricate patterns. Another trademark craft of the city was damascened steel sword blades. Damascened steel has been etched or inlaid with wavy patterns of silver or gold. Damask silk and damascened steel are still highly prized today.

The Shiite Martyr

Today, al-Husayn, the caliph named by the Shiites in 680, is remembered by Shiites as a martyr to their cause. His burial site in Karbala, in present-day southwestern Iraq, is considered a holy site by Shiites. Each year, on the first day of Muharram (the first month of the Islamic calendar), Shiite Muslims commemorate Husayn's death in battle against rival Sunni caliph Yazid. The 10-day period of mourning includes acts of repentance, self-flagellation (beating), mourning processions, and a play about Husayn's death called the *taziya*.

Muawiya had been the governor of Damascus, and he chose to make that city his capital. Damascus was one of the first major cities to be captured by the Muslims, in 635. Under Muawiya and later Umayyad caliphs, Damascus was transformed into a vibrant and thriving capital city. Over the years, it would come to be known as the "pearl of the east" and the "city of many pillars." Despite the beauty and culture of Damascus, Muawiya's decision to relocate the capital was controversial. Many Muslims believed Medina, the city of Muhammad, was the true heart of the empire.

For nearly a century, the Umayyads controlled the Islamic Empire from Damascus. During their reign, the empire grew to its largest size. Beginning with Muawiya, the Muslims expanded their conquests farther into North Africa, Western Europe, and Central Asia. By the time the Umayyads were finished, the empire stretched across three continents, from the Atlantic Ocean to the Indus River Valley in what is now Pakistan.

Despite the expansion of the empire and the prosperity that went along with it, the reign of the Umayyad rulers was not smooth. The Shiites did not support the dynasty, and continued to believe that the descendants of Muhammad, through the fourth rightly guided caliph, Ali, should be the leaders of Islam. They created the title of *imam* to honor the male descendants of Muhammad, and the imams were their true spiritual and political leaders, not the caliphs. (Not every descendant of Muhammad was an imam, but only men from a certain line. In addition, each imam was specifically named by the man who came before him.)

THE UMAYYAD DYNASTY

Before Muawiya's death, he arranged for his son Yazid to succeed him. To many Muslims, this action was shocking. Caliphs had always been chosen by respected leaders of the community. By naming his son to follow in his footsteps, Muawiya was founding a royal dynasty.

When Muawiya died in 680, the Second Civil War broke out. Conquest of other lands came to a halt as supporters of Muawiya's descendants battled supporters of Ali's descendants. The Umayyads, of course, supported Yazid (d. 683). But Yazid died just three years after his father. So another Umayyad relative, Abd al-Malik ibn Marwan (647–705), was put forward as the next caliph.

The Shiites had a different caliph in mind, however. They named Ali's son, al-Husayn (627–680). In 680, Husayn led the Shiites in battle against Yazid and the Sunnis at Karbala in Iraq. The Umayyads and their troops massacred Husayn, his family, and followers. Only two of Husayn's children escaped the slaughter. The event marked the permanent separation between the Shiites and Sunnis.

The Shiites were not the only ones who were dissatisfied with the Umayyad dynasty. Many Muslims felt the Umayyads were too "royal" and that this was not compatible with the teachings of Muhammad. One opposition group was led by Abddullah ibn al-Zubayr (d. 692), the son of one of Muhammad's companions. Ibn al-Zubayr took control of Mecca and declared himself the caliph. He attracted many followers—and this split caused the Second Civil War to drag on.

The war continued for 12 years. Soldiers, supplies, and weapons were used to wage this internal conflict, rather than to expand the empire. By 692, Abd al-Malik had taken firm control of the Islamic Empire, crushing any opposition. After recapturing Mecca, Abd al-Malik's

IN THEIR OWN WORDS

A Call to Battle

The Battle of Guadalete took place in 711 at the mouth of the Guadalete River on the southern tip of the Iberian Peninsula. Just before the battle, Muslim general Tariq ibn Ziyad ordered his soldiers to burn their boats to ensure they would fight to the death. He then made a stirring speech:

Oh my warriors, whither [where] would you flee? Behind you is the sea, before you, the enemy. You have left now only the hope of your courage and your constancy. . . . Your enemy is before you, protected by an innumerable army; he has men in abundance, but you, as your only aid, have your own swords, and, as your only chance for life, such chance as you can snatch from the hands of your enemy. . . . Do not imagine that your fate can be separated from mine, and rest assured that if you fall, I shall perish with you, or avenge you. . . . Remember that I place myself in the front of this glorious charge which I exhort you to make. At the moment when the two armies meet hand to hand, you will see me, never doubt it . . .

The Muslims were victorious in the battle, defeating a much larger force.

(Source: Horne, Charles F. *The Sacred Books and Early Literature of the East.* New York: Parke, Austin & Lipscomb, 1917.)

The Berbers

The Berbers, semi-nomadic people of North Africa, strongly resisted any efforts to convert them to Islam. When they finally did embrace Islam, however, they proved to be fierce fighters. Berber armies were instrumental in helping the Muslims conquer Spain. These Berber conquerors of Spain came to be known as the Moors. Later, the Berbers supported the kingdoms that sprang up in North Africa to rival the caliphate in Baghdad.

The term *Barbary Coast*, a section of North Africa's shoreline, was derived from the word *Berber*. Beginning in the 16th century, Berber and Arab pirates terrorized European trading ships that sailed along this stretch of ocean. Today, the Berbers are a significant part of the population in Morocco and Algeria.

forces killed Ibn al-Zubayr and sent his head to the caliph in Damascus. Until 750, Umayyad caliphs would rule the empire.

With the civil war finally at an end, the Muslims turned again to conquering new lands. This second phase of conquest served a number of important purposes. First, it enabled the empire to grow and expand. Soldiers eagerly signed on for the new conquests, hoping for wealth or a place in heaven. Second, the battles with enemies outside the empire turned the focus of the Muslims away from the problems at home. Third, the conquests were the perfect way to spread Islam.

The new conquests were extensive. More of Africa fell, enabling the Muslims to advance to the coast of Morocco. From there, an army made up largely of Berbers from North Africa began a push into Spain in 711. The troops were led by general Tariq ibn Ziyad, who took control of the southeastern two-thirds of the Iberian Peninsula.

Bows and arrows, as well as swords, were still the weapons of choice. But the Umayyad armies of conquest were very different from the raiding parties that had attacked Meccan caravans during the time of Muhammad. The armies were highly organized, and were separated by tribe into divisions. The Muslims adapted the fighting techniques of their enemies, and stayed tightly together. Fourteenth-century Arab historian Ibn Khaldun (quoted in John Jandora's *Militarism in Arab Society*) explained why the early Umayyad armies favored a closed attack formation: "They sought to die in holy war because they wished to persevere and were firm in their faith. The advance in close order is more appropriate for seeking death."

One of the chief aims of the second wave of conquests was to capture Constantinople, the capital of the Byzantine Empire, which was Christian.

Earlier caliphs had unsuccessfully tried to conquer the city. Now, under the caliph Sulayman (715–717), the Muslims tried again. From 716 to 717, Islamic troops laid siege to the city. The attacks were very costly—the

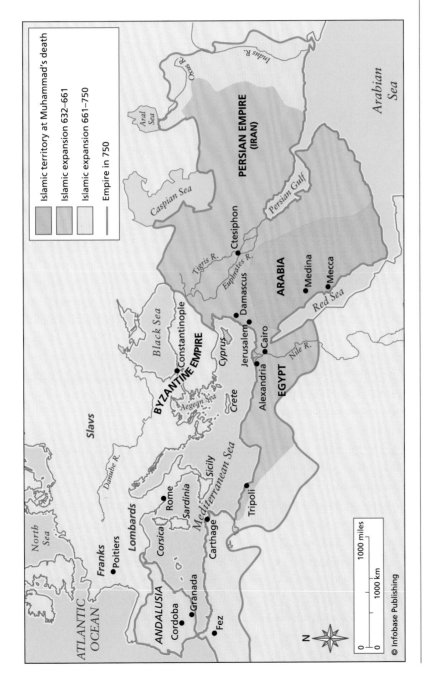

Under the reign of the Umayyad caliphs, the Islamic Empire expanded across Europe, Africa, and Asia, reaching its largest size. The end of the dynasty in 750 also marked the end of Islamic conquests.

Map labels:

Islamic territory at Muhammad's death
Islamic expansion 632–661
Islamic expansion 661–750
Empire in 750

Oxus R.
Indus R.
Aral Sea
PERSIAN EMPIRE (IRAN)
Arabian Sea
Caspian Sea
Persian Gulf
Tigris R.
Ctesiphon
Euphrates R.
ARABIA
Medina
Mecca
Red Sea
Damascus
Black Sea
Constantinople
BYZANTINE EMPIRE
Cyprus
Jerusalem
Cairo
Alexandria
Nile R.
EGYPT
Aegean Sea
Crete
Slavs
Danube R.
Mediterranean Sea
Sicily
Tripoli
North Sea
Lombards
Rome
Sardinia
Corsica
Carthage
Franks
Poitiers
ANDALUSIA
Cordoba
Granada
Fez
ATLANTIC OCEAN

1000 miles
1000 km
N
© Infobase Publishing

This illustration from an 11th-century manuscript shows the Muslims besieging the city of Messina in Sicily. They eventually captured the city.

Islamic fleet and army from Syria were wiped out. In the end the attempts to take Constantinople were not successful. Throughout the history of the Islamic Empire, Constantinople remained outside of Islamic control (although it later fell to the Muslims under the Ottoman Empire during the 15th century).

From Spain, the Muslim armies pushed across the Pyrenees, a mountain range in Europe that separates Spain from France. In 732, the Muslim advance was stopped near the Loire River in southeastern France by Charles Martel (ca. 688–741). Charles was the leader of the Franks, a people who lived in parts of modern Germany, France, and the Netherlands. This marked the farthest extent of the Islamic Empire in Europe.

Despite their failure on this front, the Muslims in 827 began raiding Sicily and southern Italy, as well as the Mediterranean coastal regions of France and Italy known as the Riviera. Here, the Muslims were more successful. They held Sicily until the middle of the 11th century.

In the East, the Muslim armies pushed from Iran into central Asia, to an area just south of the Aral Sea that is now Uzbekistan. They also moved into the Indus River Valley. Muhammad ibn al-Qasim, a 17-year-old general, took his troops from southern Iran to Daibul, the biggest city in the Indus delta. From here, they went to conquer cities in what is now Pakistan.

Despite the enlargement of the empire, opposition to the Umayyads continued to grow in the late eighth century. Many Muslims were opposed to economic changes made by the Umayyad caliphs. The Umayyads also spent vast amounts of money building and furnishing luxurious palaces. Special treatment for Umayyad relatives and friends continued to anger many.

Although later Umayyad caliphs tried to address the economic and social issues facing the empire, they generally were unsuccessful. By this time, most people were so dissatisfied with the Umayyads that they were ready for a bigger change.

The Shiites continued to stage uprisings against the Umayyad rulers. The most powerful opposition group, however, was the Abbasids in eastern Persia. The Abbasids were descendants of al-Abbas (d. 652), an uncle of Muhammad. They launched a massive propaganda campaign against the Umayyads. Using groups of people who hated the ruling caliph, they put out the word that the Umayyads were too royal and not religious enough. The Abbasids also spread the message that *they* were the true successors of Muhammad, not the Umayyads. The Abbasids managed to unite the various opposition groups against the ruling dynasty, asking for support for the true "family of Muhammad."

In 747, the Abbasids and other Umayyad enemies united under a black banner and rebelled against the Umayyads. The Abbasid revolution lasted three years. When the fighting was over, the Abbasids and their allies had put an end to the Umayyad dynasty that had lasted through 90 years and 14 caliphs.

The Abbasids were not quite finished with the Umayyads, however. After their victory, the new rulers invited 80 Umayyad leaders to a huge banquet. During this "feast of peace," hired assassins suddenly attacked the guests, bludgeoning them to death with clubs. The Abbasids threw leather covers over the dead and dying and continued eating their dinner. From this point on, the first Abbasid caliph called himself *al-saffah*, which means "blood shedder" in Arabic.

One of the Umayyad princes managed to escape the massacre. Abd al-Rahman (r. 756–788) soon founded a dynasty in Spain that rivaled the Abbasids in glory and power. In fact, after the fall of the Umayyad dynasty, the

CONNECTIONS

Geography in Spain

Muslim territory in Spain was known as al-Andalus. Today, the region is known as Andalusia, and a type of horse that originated in Spain is known as the Andalusian.

The Strait of Gibraltar, located between Africa and Spain, is named in honor of the Berber general Tariq ibn Ziyad. In 711, Tariq crossed the 13-mile-wide body of water, landing on the large rock that also bears his name: In Arabic, the rock is called Jabal Tariq (Gibraltar), which means "mount of Tariq."

This ivory jar was carved in 968 for Prince al-Mughira, son of the caliph Abd al-Rahman III of Cordoba. It is typical of the luxury goods that were common at court. The jar shows a variety of people and animals. In this scene, two figures sit next to a musician. One figure holds a fan, the other a bottle (an emblem often associated with the king).

cultural, religious, and economic connections within the Islamic Empire remained, but politically the empire was never totally unified.

THE ABBASID DYNASTY

The first Abbasid caliph was Abu al-Abbas al-Saffah (d. 754), the man who had masterminded the Abbasid revolution. His first few years as caliph were spent crushing any resistance or rivalry. Anyone who had helped the Abbasids gain power had therefore proven themselves willing to challenge the caliph. So these supporters were killed to prevent them from stirring up any more trouble in the future. This included the Shiites, who had been so important to Abbasid victory during the revolution.

By 756, new leaders were firmly in control of the Islamic Empire. The Abbasid dynasty ruled the empire for the next five centuries, until it fell in 1258.

Under the Abbasids, the capital of the empire moved from Damascus in today's Syria to Baghdad in what is now Iraq. In 762, the second Abbasid caliph, Abu Jafar al-Mansur (d. 775), founded Baghdad. The new city signaled not just an end to the old Umayyad dynasty, but a beginning of Abbasid power and glory. Baghdad remained the empire's capital—as well as its political and cultural heart—for nearly 500 years.

The beginning of the Abbasid dynasty also signaled an end to the age of Islamic conquest. The empire at the time stretched from Spain in the west to the borders of India in the east, from central Asia in the north to North Africa in the south. It entered a period of peace and prosperity, a "golden age" of Islamic civilization. Despite many advances in culture and learning, however, the Abbasids would soon lose control over their empire. A new age was coming, and it would not be long before the dynasty was reduced to nothing more than a puppet controlled by other powers within the empire.

CONNECTIONS

Watering the Desert

Under the Abbasids, the huge Islamic Empire needed to find ways to increase the production of food crops. Agriculture became a major concern. Islamic scientists translated and studied Greek and other ancient texts on farming, and they also added new knowledge to the field.

The demand for an increase in the variety and amount of new food crops led to a serious need for good irrigation and water management techniques. Islamic scholars and farmers rose to the occasion. Coming from a dry, desert climate, the Arabs always understood the importance of making effective and efficient use of available water.

In Spain, the Umayyads introduced scientific methods of irrigation borrowed from the Egyptians, including water wheels, canals, reservoirs, and pumps. As agriculture flourished throughout the region, Spain quickly earned the reputation as the garden of Europe. Other scientific methods of farming introduced into Spain included the use of new fertilizers to help crops grow; knowledge about growing varieties of trees and plant diseases; cross pollination of plants; and soil rehabilitation.

CHAPTER 3

THE LAST YEARS OF THE EMPIRE

LIKE THE UMAYYADS BEFORE THEM, THE ABBASIDS FACED the hostility and resentment of the Shiites. Although the Shiites had helped the Abbasids take control of the empire, the Abbasids had not been grateful. Throughout the following years, the relationship between the Abbasids and the Shiites alternated between tolerance and persecution.

There was also fighting and conflict within the Abbasids' own family. Because they did not practice primogeniture (in which the oldest son inherits his father's land and title), the Abbasid caliphs could name anyone they wanted to succeed them. The result was that different groups within the family supported certain brothers, sons, or other male relatives for control of the empire. There was much fighting and little trust between the Abbasid relatives.

In 809, a bloody civil war erupted between two Abbasid half-brothers, al-Amin (d. 813) and al-Mamun (786–833). Although al-Amin had been chosen by his father, the caliph Harun al-Rashid, al-Mamun wanted control of the empire. Al-Mamun killed al-Amin in 813, but the civil war continued for six more years.

As time went by, the bitter family fighting—and the huge size of the empire itself—weakened the dynasty. Several areas split off from the control of the caliph. They became states that governed themselves. Spain and North Africa are two examples of regions that had their own local dynasties or governments.

As time passed, even areas that were still supposedly under the control of the Abbasid caliphs were actually ruled by local governors, tribes, or strong families. In 820, for example, a general named Tahir (ca. 798–ca. 845) who had been appointed governor of Khurasan in Persia claimed control of the region. Soon, other Persian governors were following his lead.

Even though they claimed loyalty to the Abbasids, they functioned as separate states. By 836, things were so bad for the caliph in Baghdad that he moved the capital of his empire 60 miles up the Tigris River to Samarra, for safety.

By the 940s, the Abbasid caliphs held symbolic authority as religious leaders, but they had lost all control of the political, military, and governmental power of the empire. This situation continued until the destruction of Baghdad in 1258.

In 945, the first of the Abbasids' "protectors" began running the empire. These were strong military men who actually ruled, while the weak caliphs kept their titles. Muizz al-Dawla, a member of the powerful Buyid family from northwestern Iran, took control of Baghdad and was named commander in chief. The Buyids replaced the Turkish guards who had previously been in control.

The Buyids divided up the empire, granting various brothers and cousins control of different regions. Soon, the Buyids, like the Abbasids, were competing with one another to take full control of the Abbasids and their empire. While some regions were very well run and grew into thriving centers of business, trade, and culture, others were not. The Buyids managed to remain the protectors of the Abbasids until 1055, when the Seljuk Turks took over what was left of the Islamic Empire.

The challenges the ruling Abbasids faced from within their own empire made it easier for those outside of the empire to begin attacking and chipping away at Muslim territories. The first outside challenge to Islamic power came in the early 11th century from the Turkmen, tribes of semi-nomadic Turkish-speaking people.

Around that time, famine caused the Turkmen to begin migrating into northern Iran. As they moved into Muslim-held areas, the Turkmen defeated area tribes, taking control of the region. Eventually one group of Turkmen, the Seljuk Turks, became powerful enough to become the Abbasid caliphs' new "protectors."

Like the Buyids before them, the Seljuks kept the Abbasids on as religious leaders, allowing them to keep the title of caliph. The Seljuks themselves took the title of sultan, as well as King of the East and the West. The title sultan emphasizes the fact that the ruler had political authority but was not head of the Islamic community—which the title caliph implied. At the time of the Buyids and Seljuks, this meant the sultans were appointed by the caliph. But in reality, the sultans had the power. Seljuk control of the empire marked the start of a strong Turkish influence and the decline of Arab influence.

Under the Seljuk Turks, Islamic conquest was taken up once again. The Seljuks eventually advanced into other areas that were controlled by the Byzantine Empire, laying the foundation for the Ottoman Empire and, later, modern Turkey. They also brought Islam to these areas.

SPAIN SPLITS OFF

By the time the Seljuk Turks took control of the empire, other areas had long ago separated themselves from Abbasid control. One of the first regions to split off was Spain. In 755, Abd al-Rahman (the Umayyad prince who had escaped being murdered when the Abbasids took control in 747) fled to North Africa. He eventually reached Spain and took over, setting up his own Umayyad state there.

At first, the rulers of this new dynasty called themselves emir, which is Arabic for "commander." This meant that they accepted the Abbasid rulers as the caliphs of the empire. But in the late 920s, things changed. Abd al-Rahman III (891–961) claimed for himself the title of caliph.

To celebrate his self-appointed title, Abd al-Rahman III established his capital at Madinat al-Zahra, three miles west of Cordoba. The magnificent city included a mosque, palace, government offices, markets, public baths, and beautiful gardens. The caliph offered silver coins to anyone who would settle in his new city.

Madinat al-Zahra was built into the hillside, and the high and low buildings reflected the high and low status of the various people in the social structure. The caliph lived on the highest of three levels. Government officials lived and worked on the second level. Soldiers and the rest of the citizens lived on the lowest level, near the markets and bath houses. Under the Umayyads, Spain remained a center of Islamic culture until 1031. At that time, it was divided into a number of Muslim city-states (cities that, with their surrounding territory, form independent states). To prevent the Catholic kings in northern Spain from conquering Muslim areas, the city-states invited the Almoravids, Berber rulers from Morocco, to take control around 1085. For more than 100

The Alhambra

Even though it was built mostly after the fall of the Abbasid dynasty, the Alhambra, a palace in Granada, Spain, showcases Islamic architecture at its height. The palace was built by the Nasrid sultans, who ruled southern Spain until 1492. The magnificent palace includes the ornamentation that Islamic builders were famous for, including columns, pillars, archways, fountains, and domes. Magnificent gardens connect the various buildings above ground, and cool, restful bath houses connect them below. One dome contains thousands of plaster stalactites that hang from the ceiling, making it look like a cave. Today, the Alhambra is a tourist attraction.

The Alhambra towers over Granada. Today, it is a major tourist attraction.

years, Almoravid and Almohad (another group of Muslim Berbers) rulers controlled the area.

Muslim territory in Spain was known as al-Andalus. Granada, the last Muslim stronghold in al-Andalus, which was ruled from 1232 by the Nasrid Dynasty, was taken in 1492 by the army of Catholic rulers Ferdinand (1452–1516) and Isabella (1451–1504) of Spain. The Spanish king and queen immediately set about restoring Christianity to their land. They gave Muslims the option to convert or return to North Africa. Any Muslim who chose to remain a Muslim and stay in Spain was hunted down and killed. In an effort to wipe out all traces of Islam in Granada, more than 1 million Arabic books were burned in the public square. By the early 1500s, the Inquisition (a special religious court that had begun in 1478 to forcibly eliminate any unorthodox religious thinking), had turned its attention from converted Jews to the Muslims. Muslim who had managed to escape the first waves of forced baptism or execution were now subjected to a second attack.

CONNECTIONS

Muslim Influence in Spain

At the height of the Islamic Empire, the Arabs controlled the southeastern two-thirds of the Iberian Peninsula. The Muslims revitalized such Spanish cities as Cordoba, Toledo, Granada, and Seville. For more than five centuries, Spain was a unique place in Europe, a region where culture and learning were valued and encouraged.

By 1248, when Seville was conquered by Christian forces, the Muslims had lost control of all of Spain except Granada. At first the conquerors did not expel all the Muslims. By about 1500 though, after the fall of Granada, things had changed. In their attempts to wipe out all traces of Muslim influence, the Christian conquerors banned the Arabic language. Muslims in Spain were faced with the choice of converting to Christianity or leaving forever.

Despite this, Islamic influences can still be found throughout the region. For example, many Arabic words are part of the Spanish language. The Spanish expression *olé* comes from the Arabic *wallahi*, which means "by God!" Many other Spanish words that begin with "al" have Arabic origins, including *alcachofa* (artichoke), *aldea* (village), and *aljibe* (well).

Visitors can also see signs of Muslim control in Spanish architecture. The Alhambra in Granada and the Giralda Tower in Seville are two examples of the influence of Islamic style on the Iberian Peninsula. Many homes in southern Spain still retain such Muslim architectural touches as the use of whitewashed, windowless outer walls and central courtyards.

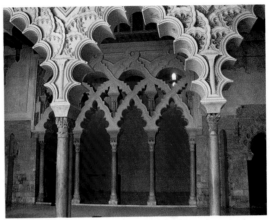

One type of design that was popular in the Islamic Empire was a swirling, interlocking pattern of spirals inspired by the way plants, leaves, and stems wound around each other. This type of pattern became known as arabesque. Arabesques were first used to decorate mosques, and later were also used on chests, rugs, tombs, and the walls of private homes. These arabesques decorate the arches of the Alhambra.

Many important goods were introduced to Europe via Muslim Spain. Sugar cane, cotton, rice, almonds, cured meats, and many types of fruits and vegetables all first came to Europe thanks to the Muslim conquerors.

One of Muslim Spain's key contributions to Europe was the introduction of paper. The production of paper spread from China to the Middle East, then onward to Spain, Italy, and the rest of Europe. Papermaking enabled people to produce books more cheaply, and encouraged the spread of learning and knowledge throughout Europe.

NORTH AFRICA AND THE FATIMIDS

From the earliest days of the Islamic Empire, the more distant areas of Africa were under less direct control from the caliph and the central government. Additionally, many Berbers were converted by the Kharijites, who were outside the mainstream of Sunni Islam and always opposed the reigning caliphs. As a result, separate Islamic states were set up in what are now Libya, Tunisia, and Algeria. Soon, the Kharijite groups had spread to modern-day Chad, Niger, and Mali.

The first of these separate Islamic African kingdoms was established around 800. At this time, the Abbasid caliph was forced to recognize North African governor Ibrahim ibn al-Aghlab as hereditary governor. This meant the office of governor could be passed on to his relatives and the caliph would not appoint him. For the next 100 years, the Aghlabids ruled the area and barely acknowledged the Abbasids as caliphs.

The most powerful Islamic kingdom in Africa was run by the Fatimids, a Shiite family originally from southwestern Persia. The Fatimids took control of North Africa in 909. The family was headed by Ubayd Allah (871–934). He claimed to be descended from Ali's wife Fatima, who was Muhammad's daughter. The Fatimids believed Ubayd Allah was the rightful caliph of the whole Islamic Empire. He also claimed to be the Mahdi, Arabic for "the rightly-guided one." According to some Islamic traditions, the Mahdi will come before the end of time to restore Islam to its original perfection.

After taking control of North Africa with the help of Berber tribes, the Fatimids gave themselves the title of caliph. In 914, they founded a new capital called Mahdiyah (in what is now Tunisia). Although the Fatimids hated the Abbasids, they laid out their towns in much the same way as Baghdad had been designed—in a circular pattern with the palace at its center.

The Fatimid caliphs took the idea of royalty to an extreme. Anything the caliph touched was considered sacred. His clothing or even the sight of him was considered to have *baraka*, or grace, which was passed on to anyone who saw him or came in contact with him. The caliph was also thought to be able to heal the sick and bring rain to dry areas.

The Fatimids faced internal opposition, but managed to hold onto power for two centuries. One of their major accomplishments was taking control of Egypt in 969 (although, soon after, they lost control of Tunisia and other lands farther to the west). The loss of Egypt, which was a rich, money-making province, was a serious blow to the Abbasids.

Saladin in Film

Kingdom of Heaven is a 2005 movie about the Crusades that was directed by Ridley Scott (who also directed *Blackhawk Down* and *Gladiator*). The story takes place in the 1180s. Balian (played by Orlando Bloom), a French blacksmith, goes to Jerusalem to fight against the Muslims, lead by Saladin (referred to in the East as Salah al-Din). Ghassan Massoud, a Syrian actor, played Saladin. Most of the filming was done in Morocco and Spain. A replica of the ancient city of Jerusalem was also constructed in the desert.

Sicily

Sicily was the only other region in Europe (besides Spain) that the Islamic Empire managed to conquer and control for a significant period of time. Aghlabids, Muslim Berbers from North Africa, first captured Sicily in 827. In 909, the Fatimids defeated the Aghlabids and took control of Sicily and North Africa.

Under Islamic control, Palermo became a center of culture, knowledge, and commerce. It was famous for sugar, flax, olives, and silk weaving. By the 11th century, the island had about 300 mosques, according to contemporary Muslim reports.

When the Normans (people from Normandy, a region in what is today northwestern France) conquered the region after about 250 years of Muslim rule, they were impressed with the island's sophisticated culture.

Unlike the Catholics in Spain, the Normans did not try to get rid of all Muslim influences in Sicily. The Norman ruler, Roger (ca. 1031–1101), allowed Muslims to continue practicing their religion, welcomed Muslim soldiers into his army, and embraced Muslim scholars. On the day he was crowned, the new king of Sicily wore a robe with Arabic words stitched into it. He also continued to follow the Islamic calendar.

The Muslim cultural influence in Sicily continued for centuries. Frederick II of Sicily (1272–1337), who later became Holy Roman Emperor, dressed in Muslim fashions and kept a harem (a group of women, usually relatives including multiple wives, who lived in a secluded part of the house). Arab scholars and administrators were a key part of his court, and Arabic was one of the four official Sicilian languages. It was at Frederick's University of Naples that St. Thomas Aquinas, an important Christian scholar, first read Arabic translations of classical Greek texts.

The Fatimids established the city of Cairo (now the capital of Egypt) and founded al-Azhar University, which is the oldest continuously open university in the world.

From 975 to 1036, the Fatimid caliphs were the most powerful in the Islamic Empire. At one point the Friday prayers in Mecca and Medina were actually changed, offering blessings to the Fatimid caliph in Egypt instead of the Abbasid caliph in Baghdad.

Although they enjoyed support in many areas of the kingdom, the Fatimids were not recognized in Baghdad. Their dynasty eventually weakened. In the 11th century they were defeated by the Seljuk Turks, who were now the "protectors" of the Abbasid dynasty.

Al-Azhar Mosque and University in Cairo, Egypt, is one of the oldest universities in the world. The mosque and university are named in honor of Fatima al-Zahraa, the daughter of Muhammad, from whom the Fatimid dynasty is descended. The mosque was built in two years, beginning in ca. 971 C.E.

By 1073 the once-powerful Fatimids were in the same position as their Abbasid enemies: reduced to puppets under the control of powerful government officials and military commanders. In 1171, Kurdish military leader Saladin (1138–1193), known in the East as Salah al-Din, seized control of Egypt and brought an end to the Fatimid dynasty. He declared himself the sultan of Egypt and founded the Ayyubid dynasty.

Saladin's descendants controlled Egypt until 1250, when Turkish slave soldiers called the Mamluks took control. The Mamluks were the last great dynasty of the Islamic Empire.

THE CRUSADES

In 1095, Pope Urban II (ca. 1042–1099) called on all good Christians to retake the Holy Land (the area of the Middle East that is sacred to Christians and Jews), particularly the city of Jerusalem, from the

Muslims. He said that because these sites were holy to Christians, God wanted Christians to control them. More than 30,000 Europeans responded, and set out for the Middle East on the First Crusade.

On the way to Jerusalem, the crusaders captured the Muslim regions of what are now Syria, Lebanon, and Israel. They established a number of "crusader kingdoms," which were small states controlled by the Christian conquerors.

The most important crusader kingdom was the Latin Kingdom of Jerusalem, which the Christians captured in 1099. When they entered Jerusalem, the Christian soldiers showed themselves to be far less merciful than the conquering Muslims had been. Crusaders slaughtered the Muslims and Jews of the city. They even killed the Eastern

IN THEIR OWN WORDS

Crusaders Needed

In 1095, Alexios I Komnenos, the Byzantine emperor, asked Pope Urban II for help from the west to fight the Seljuk Turks. At the Council of Clermont in France, Urban urged the large crowd that had gathered to help Alexios recover Palestine from Muslim rule. The result was the First Crusade.

Urban's speech was written down by five men who were present and heard him. Each version is different. This is from the account by the chronicler (someone who collects and writes down history) Fulcher of Chartres.

For, as the most of you have heard, the Turks and Arabs have attacked them and have conquered the territory of Romania [the Greek empire]. . . . They have killed and captured many, and have destroyed the churches and devastated the empire. . . . On this account I, or rather the Lord, beseech you as Christ's heralds to publish this everywhere and to persuade

all people of whatever rank, foot-soldiers and knights, poor and rich, to carry aid promptly to those Christians and to destroy that vile race from the lands of our friends. I say this to those who are present, it meant also for those who are absent. Moreover, Christ commands it.

Just as Muslims who died for their faith were promised entrance into paradise, Urban promised Christians that their sins would be forgiven:

All who die by the way, whether by land or by sea, or in battle against the pagans, shall have immediate remission of sins. This I grant them through the power of God with which I am invested.

(Source: Fulcher of Chartres. "Gesta Francorum Jerusalem Expugnantium." Thatcher, Oliver J., and Edgar Holmes, editors. *A Source Book for Medieval History,* New York: Charles Scribner and Sons, 1905.)

The Battle of Dorylaeum, between the crusaders and the Seljuk Turks, is illustrated in this 14th-century French book. The battle took place in Anatolia (modern Turkey) in 1097. The crusaders won.

Christians, whom the Roman Catholic Church considered to be outside mainstream Christianity.

Christian control of the Holy Land did not last long. In 1188, Saladin took back Jerusalem. Over the coming years, he and his successors regained control of the other crusader kingdoms. The last crusader kingdom fell in 1291.

The Crusades had more significance for Europe than they did for the people of the Islamic Empire. For the people of Islam, the Crusades were merely routine conflicts for control of various regions. In fact, most people of the Islamic Empire looked upon the crusaders as invaders from a civilization much cruder and less advanced than their own.

One unanticipated effect of the Crusades was that they helped spread Islamic goods, culture, and thought to Europe. Not only did the crusaders learn Islamic military techniques (including the use of pigeons to carry messages), but they also brought home goods that soon became very popular, including spices, foods, and textiles. More luxurious goods brought from the East included rugs, glass mirrors, cosmetics, dyes, and soap.

THE MONGOLS

The challengers who would ultimately bring an end to the Islamic Empire did not come from Europe. Rather, they swept down on horseback from central Asia. In the early 1200s, a Mongol leader named Chinggis Khan (ca. 1162–1227; his name is sometimes written as Genghis Khan) and his family conquered most of what are today China, Russia, Iran, Turkey, and

Iraq. Chinggis Khan began his raids into Islamic territory in 1219. He established himself in what is now Uzbekistan and worked his way south into northern Persia. In 1256, Chinggis Khan's grandson Hülegü (ca. 1217–1265) continued further through Persia and into Iraq.

IN THEIR OWN WORDS

The Capture of Jerusalem

In 1188, Saladin retook Jerusalem from the Christian crusaders. Eventually, he took over most of the other crusader kingdoms as well. In 1191, he met Britain's King Richard I (1157–1199), also known as Richard the Lionhearted, in battle. Saladin was the victor.

This account of Saladin's conquest of Jerusalem is part of a British history called *Chronicon Anglicanum*. It was compiled by Ralph of Coggeshall, a monk who was one of the most important historians of early 13th-century Britain. The actual description of events is an eyewitness account from a soldier who took part in the defense of Jerusalem and was wounded. He refers to the Muslims as "Turkish" and "Saracens."

> *The Holy City of Jerusalem was besieged on September 20. It was surrounded on every side by unbelievers, who shot arrows everywhere into the air. They were accompanied by frightening armaments and, with a great clamor of trumpets, they shrieked and wailed, "Hai, hai." . . .*

> *The battle was then joined and both sides began courageously to fight. But since so much unhappiness was produced through sorrow and sadness, we shall not enumerate all the Turkish attacks and assemblies, by which, for two weeks, the Christians were worn down. . . . There were so many wounded that all the hospitals and physicians in the city were hard put to it just to extract the missiles from their bodies. I myself was wounded in the face by an arrow which struck the bridge of my nose. The wooden shaft has been taken out, but the metal tip has remained there to this day. . . .*

> *But, alas, by the hands of wicked Christians Jerusalem was turned over to the wicked. . . . The ministers of the wicked error, who are considered bishops and priests by the Saracens, came for prayer and religious purposes first to the Temple of the Lord. . . . They believed they were cleansing it and with unclean and horrible bellows they defiled the Temple by shouting with polluted lips the Muslim precept: "Allahu akbar! Allahu akbar! [God is great]"*

(Source: *De Expugatione Terrae Sanctae per Saladinum* (The capture of the Holy Land by Saladin). Brundage, James A., translator. *The Crusades: A Documentary Survey.* Milwaukee, Wisc.: Marquette University Press, 1962.)

CONNECTIONS

The Origin of Assassins

The Assassins was a secret organization, a radical branch of the Sevener Shiites. The group was started around 1090 by a Persian who claimed to be descended from tribal kings in southern Arabia.

The Assassins had their headquarters in the mountains of northern Iran. From there, the group raided and took control of other fortresses. The Assassins also became known for their bloody methods of getting rid of those who stood in their way. Targets were often prominent Sunni political or religious leaders. The Assassins' favorite method of killing was the dagger, a short knife.

The term *assassin* comes from the Arabic word *hashshash*, which, translated literally, means a person who uses hashish—a mind-altering drug. Legend has it that some of the lower members of the group, the ones who performed the actual killings, were controlled by other members through the use of hashish. However, *hashshash* can also mean a useless person. Today, an assassin is someone who murders a politically prominent person.

The Mongol conquests were extremely destructive. Cities and their residents were wiped out and irrigation projects destroyed, which ruined the farming of the region.

In 1258 Hülegü entered Baghdad itself. Here, the Mongol soldiers massacred thousands of people and the caliph's palace was destroyed. The caliph, his family, and his officials were also killed to make sure no one remained to claim control. By 1260, most of the Islamic east was under Mongol control and the Islamic Empire was no more.

PART·II

SOCIETY AND CULTURE

SOCIETY IN THE ISLAMIC EMPIRE

LIVING IN THE ISLAMIC EMPIRE

ISLAMIC ART, SCIENCE, AND CULTURE

CHAPTER 4

SOCIETY IN THE ISLAMIC EMPIRE

AS THE ISLAMIC EMPIRE GREW AND EXPANDED, ITS government had to change to meet the needs of the changing situation. The different styles of government and leadership throughout the history of the empire reflect the efforts of caliphs to maintain control of the wide variety of lands and people they ruled.

THE CALIPHATE AND THE UMAYYAD DYNASTY

The first government of the Islamic Empire was centered on the caliph, who was considered the successor of Muhammad. The caliph was both the spiritual and political leader of the empire. His authority as the supreme leader of the *umma* was not questioned.

The government was an Islamic theocracy—a government in which religious rulers govern in the name of God. There was no separation of religion and government. The laws of the empire were based on the Quran, the example set by Muhammad, and the rulings of the caliph.

Sunni Muslims believed the first four rightly guided caliphs set the example for all caliphs. They were all Arabs from Muhammad's tribe and most of them were chosen by a council of leaders who represented the entire *umma*.

After the first four caliphs, however, this example was rarely followed. That is why although the Umayyad leaders continued to call themselves caliphs, some experts consider the Umayyad dynasty more like a kingdom.

Muawiya, the first Umayyad caliph, made his dynasty like a kingdom by establishing a line of succession and elevating the caliph and his court to a higher class in the empire's social structure. Although ordinary citizens could approach and speak to the first caliphs, Muawiya began to act in a more royal manner. He appointed a doorkeeper to decide who could or could not see the caliph.

The first Umayyad caliph also created a royal bodyguard, made up of soldiers, who accompanied him everywhere he went. Later Umayyad caliphs relied even more heavily on the military to help them keep their power.

The Umayyads were the first caliphs who had to deal with a newly expanded empire, and under them the Islamic Empire grew to its largest size. At a time when travel and communication over large distances was slow and difficult, the caliph could not personally keep firm control over all of his empire. To make sure things continued to run smoothly in the conquered lands, the local system of government was usually left in place. Then, to ensure cooperation, the caliph divided the empire into regions and appointed strong, capable governors to oversee them.

At first, governorships were awarded to the caliph's relatives or other upper class Arabs. Later, they were given to army commanders and other leaders who had demonstrated some ability. In some cases, governors were appointed for life or were allowed to pass on their position to their relatives. In most cases, however, the caliph chose to rotate the governors. In some regions, for example, the governors were replaced almost yearly. This kept them under control and ensured that they would not become too powerful.

The governor had many duties. Of course, he had to continue to recognize the caliph as the supreme leader of the empire. The governor had to raise an army and be prepared to send his troops to defend the empire whenever necessary. But the governor's most important job was to collect taxes from the citizens of his territory. These taxes were the lifeblood of the Islamic Empire. As long as revenues from the territories continued to fill the caliph's treasury, the governor was allowed to control his area the way he saw fit.

At home, the Umayyads worked to centralize government functions. They moved the heart of the new empire to Syria (Syria was the first region outside of Arabia conquered by the Muslims). From here, the caliph was able to administer and control his many provinces. In addition, the Umayyads started a number of government innovations. For example, they set up a postal service. Riders on horseback delivered messages from one part of the empire to another. The Umayyads also established a bureau of registry to record births, deaths, and other important events, and were the first Islamic rulers to mint coins in silver and gold.

THE ROYAL ABBASID DYNASTY

Although the Umayyads slowly changed the caliph into a king, the Abbasids took the concept to a whole new level. The new dynasty followed the lead of Persian royalty. They claimed to have powers from God and asserted total authority in all matters, both religious and political.

The Abbasid caliphs and their families also tried to make themselves seem more "apart" and royal by surrounding their court with mystery and ceremony. In *The Arabs in History*, Bernard Lewis says the "new dignity of the Caliph was expressed in new titles, and in a much more elaborate ceremonial."

Unlike the earliest caliphs, the Abbasid rulers held themselves and their family apart from the common people. Instead of going through a doorkeeper, as in Umayyad times, people hoping to meet with the Abbasid caliphs had to first make their pleas to a series of chamberlains (household officers).

Rulers rarely appeared in public, but when they did, they wore expensive silk robes and rare perfumes. Those who did see the caliph had to follow an elaborate routine that included kissing the ground and avoiding looking directly at the ruler.

Under the Abbasids, the government of the empire became even more efficient than it had been under the Umayyads. The early Abbasid caliphs created a centralized system of administration. Its main function was to efficiently collect, control, and spend revenues that were raised through taxation.

The bureaucracy associated with the Abbasid government was highly developed. (A bureaucracy is an administrative system with many layers and functions in which most of the important decisions are made by appointed officials, called bureaucrats.) By the middle of the ninth century, the Abbasids' administration was made up of several departments, called *diwans*. They included the treasury, the accounting department, the intelligence department, a chancery department that handled all official correspondence, and a court of appeals. Every aspect of government was handled through the *diwans* and the thousands of clerks and secretaries who worked in them.

Under the Abbasids, the importance and power of high-born Arab officials and army officers declined. Government offices and positions of authority were now awarded to those who were most capable, not those from certain families.

In the earliest days of the Abbasid dynasty, the people who had run the local government before an area was conquered continued to do the same work after the Muslims took over. In Baghdad, this meant a highly educated class of Persian officials ran day-to-day affairs. These Persian secretaries enjoyed great wealth and influence.

The caliph and his assistants also selected freed slaves and members of the previous ruler's household whom they believed were best-suited for high-ranking government positions. As a result, many Christians, Jews, and Zoroastrians were involved in the workings of the Islamic government.

The Abbasid dynasty marked the rise of *wazirs*, or viziers. Viziers were top-level administrators—professional, highly educated men who were knowledgeable in literature, writing, management, taxation, and many other areas. The Abbasid caliphs came to depend heavily on their viziers. This was especially true in the later years of the dynasty when the caliph became less involved in government and more involved in leading a life of pleasure. The viziers, many of whom were Persian, therefore became extremely powerful. During the later years of the dynasty, many viziers effectively ran the empire while the caliph served merely as a political and religious symbol.

One of the most powerful families of viziers was the Barmecides, who served the first five Abbasid caliphs. The Barmecides were Persians who had converted to Islam. The Barmecide viziers were much-beloved by the people of Baghdad, who considered them to be capable, intelligent, and generous. In the early 800s, it seemed that the Barmecide viziers had it all.

The vizier Jafar served under caliph Harun al-Rashid (766–809). As a sign of his high opinion of Jafar, the caliph allowed the vizier to marry his favorite sister, Abbasah. However, the marriage was meant to be just a symbol—Harun al-Rashid did not actually intend for them to live together as husband and wife. When Abbasah became pregnant, the end was near for the Barmecides. Jafar was eventually executed by the caliph. Harun al-Rashid also had a number of Jafar's family members imprisoned and took for himself their property and wealth.

As time went on, the huge Abbasid bureaucracy became too expensive to support. As more people around the empire converted to Islam, the amount of tax revenue decreased, because non-Muslims had to pay much higher taxes. Because of their financial problems, the Abbasid caliphs eventually required governors to pay for and maintain regional armies and bureaucracies. This strengthened the role of the governor while weakening the role of the caliph. As time went on, the governors were basically running—and ruling—their own provinces.

By the 940s, the Abbasids in Baghdad were not much more than symbols, with other groups that were known as "protectors," controlling the empire. These protectors were often army commanders who had taken advantage of the weakening caliph to grab control. Although the government structure remained the same, the caliph was now only the symbolic leader of the empire and the Islamic faith. His real power was very limited. One group of protectors was the Seljuk Turks. After they took control of the empire in 1050, they gave themselves the title of *sultan* (in Arabic the word means "power" or "ruler").

THE MILITARY

Under the first four caliphs, the army was made up of Arabs, Bedouins, and others who had volunteered to spread the word of Islam and conquer other nations. Although the early army was loosely organized, it was an important and effective fighting force in the Islamic Empire.

Being a soldier for the empire was quickly recognized as a sure way to gain land and loot. Those who took part in conquests were awarded pensions (regular payments made after a person retires) and did not have to pay the land tax required of all other landowners in the empire.

Under the Umayyads, the makeup of the army changed to include many Syrians. Under the Abbasids, many Persians entered the army. The army itself also became more streamlined and better organized. Instead of being made up of Arab volunteers from various tribes, the army was soon made up of trained units of non-Arab professional soldiers. Volunteers were still accepted, but only when they were needed.

This trend toward hiring professional soldiers started in 833, when Caliph al-Mutasim (d. 842) decided to create an army that was entirely loyal to him, with few ties to others in the community. Before, the army had been made up of separate groups commanded by strong leaders. Troops were often more loyal to their leaders than to the caliph himself.

To create an army of loyal troops, al-Mutasim recruited mostly Turks, slaves, and freed slaves. Many of the caliph's new soldiers did not even speak Arabic. To ensure that his loyal troops did not mingle

Harun al-Rashid and Charlemagne

During the early ninth century, the two most powerful rulers in the world were Caliph Harun al-Rashid in the East and Charlemagne (742–814) in the West. Charlemagne, leader of the Franks, was the grandson of Charles Martel, who had turned back the Muslim advance into France in 732. Harun al-Rashid and Charlemagne struck up a relationship and sent gifts to one another. Among the gifts the Abbasid caliph sent to Charlemagne were fabrics, perfumes, and exotic animals, including an elephant.

or become involved with Baghdad's residents, al-Mutasim built a new capital, Samarra, 60 miles north of Baghdad.

Turkish professional soldiers eventually came to dominate the army—and the empire. By 861, Turkish officers were able to decide who would become the next caliph (al-Muntasir—they later assassinated him). By the 940s, the army's commander in chief was totally in control of the empire and called himself the caliph's "protector."

SOCIAL CLASSES

The Islamic Empire, like other great civilizations before and after it, had specific social classes. Despite the fact that the Quran says all Muslims are equal, these classes existed throughout the empire.

These classes were often based on family ties—similar to the concept of royalty and nobility in the rest of the world at that time. Eventually, as non-Arabs married Arabs and family bloodlines became less distinct, the separations between some of the classes begin to blur. But that change was very slow.

Even before Muhammad and Islam, the Quraysh tribe in Mecca represented a sort of Arab aristocracy. After the Umayyad and Abbasid caliphs took control, the most elite of the upper class were made up of the rulers, their families, and their officials and those in their court, called courtiers. Under the Umayyads, those officials and courtiers were often members of the Quraysh tribe. The Umayyads themselves belonged to this tribe. Under the Abbasids, Persian officials and courtiers were also selected for top positions.

As the empire expanded, another upper-level social class appeared. This class of people was made up of the Arab descendants of Muhammad's companions, as well as the descendants of those Arabs who had taken part in the early wars of conquest. As early followers of Islam, these people received pensions, large pieces of land, and special privileges.

Below the upper class of Arab Muslims were the *mawali*, an Arabic word that means "clients." The *mawali* were new Muslims—non-Arabs who converted to Islam after being conquered. To become a *mawala* (singular of *mawali*), non-Arabs had to be accepted by an Arab patron or master, called a *mawla*. (This requirement was eventually removed by the Abbasids.)

The *mawali* were not, at first, considered the equals of Arab Muslims. Although the Quran says they should have been treated the same

way, this was not usually the case. During the Umayyad dynasty, for example, *mawali* were still taxed at a higher rate than Arab Muslims. *Mawali* in the army received lower pay than Arabs and usually had to fight as infantry soldiers. Marriages between *mawali* and Arabs were discouraged.

Over time the *mawali* population in fortified towns actually out-numbered the Arabs. As their numbers increased, the converts began to realize the enormous power they could have within the empire.

Because they disliked Umayyad economic policies, many *mawali* joined the Shiites (the Umayyads were Sunnis). It quickly became clear to the Umayyad rulers that they must find a way to satisfy this growing class of people, and economic and social reforms were the result. After Umar II became caliph in 717, for example, he changed the tax structure so the *mawali* did not have to pay the same taxes non-Muslims paid.

A third class of people in the Islamic Empire were the *dhimmis*—people who followed religions that were protected under Islam. *Dhimmis* (the Arabic word means "protected minority") included Christians and Jews, whom Muslims considered "Peoples of the Book" because they followed the word of God as revealed by prophets in the Old and New Testaments of the Judeo-Christian Bible. (Muslims recognize prophets who came before Muhammad, including Adam, Noah, Abraham, Moses, and Jesus.)

The Muslims also tolerated other monotheistic religions, including Zoroastrianism, which was widespread in Persia. People who

IN THEIR OWN WORDS

Rules for Non-Muslims

When Umar ibn al-Khattab (ca. 581–644), the second "rightly guided" caliph, conquered Syria, he made the following agreement with the Christians living there. In this document, called the Pact of Umar, the Christians agreed that in return for Umar's protection, they would follow these rules:

We shall not build, in our cities or in their neighborhood, new monasteries, Churches, convents, or monks' cells, nor shall we repair, by day or by night, such of them as fall in ruins or are situated in the quarters of the Muslims.

We shall keep our gates wide open for passersby and travelers. We shall give board and lodging to all Muslims who pass our way for three days.

We shall not give shelter in our churches or in our dwellings to any spy, nor hide him from the Muslims.

We shall not teach the Quran to our children.

We shall not manifest our religion publicly nor convert anyone to it. We shall not prevent any of our kin from entering Islam if they wish it.

We shall show respect toward the Muslims, and we shall rise from our seats when they wish to sit.

(Source: "Pact of Umar, 7th Century." Medieval Sourcebook. Available online. URL: http://www.fordham.edu/halsall/source/pact-umar.html. Accessed March 5, 2008.)

worshipped idols or multiple gods were not considered *dhimmi*. For them, the choice was to convert, leave the empire, or die.

In most parts of the empire, *dhimmis* were treated well. They often held important positions in government and owned their own businesses. They were allowed to continue practicing their religion, as well—but only in private.

Dhimmis throughout the empire were, however, under some restrictions. In addition to the land tax, which all members of the empire paid, they had to pay an extra head tax—a tax paid per person each year. In some parts of the empire, *dhimmis* had to carry certificates showing that they had indeed paid their yearly head tax.

They were forbidden to build new houses of worship and could not try to convert others to their religion. They could not worship outside their church or synagogue. They could not ride horses or carry weapons. They also had to wear distinctive clothing that signified their religion. They were not allowed to testify against a Muslim in a court of law, and they could not live in Mecca or Medina. Depending upon the current caliph, these and other restrictions might be eased or tightened.

Although the restrictions might seem designed to encourage *dhimmis* to convert to Islam, most Muslims were content to allow them to retain their own religions. The Muslims preferred having the income from the *dhimmis'* head tax.

Still, many of the conquered people began to convert to Islam. Some *dhimmis* converted for financial reasons: They no longer wanted to pay the taxes that were levied on non-Muslims.

Others, especially the poor and disadvantaged, embraced the Islamic ideas of equality and justice. In this way, Islam spread throughout a vast empire that included people of many races and beliefs.

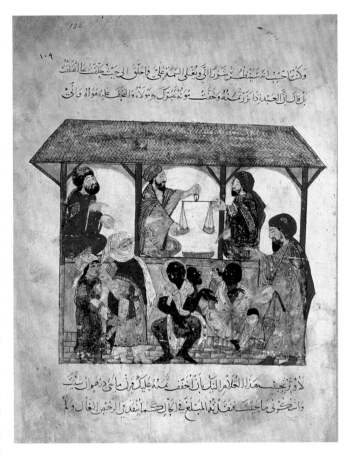

Islam permitted slavery, although Muslims were not allowed to enslave other Muslims. This scene of a slave market was made in Baghdad in 1237.

IN THEIR OWN WORDS

Freeing Slaves

This selection from the Hadith, a collection of the words and deeds of Muhammad, deals with slavery. The prophet is Muhammad and Allah is God. The word *manumission* means freeing a slave.

> I asked the Prophet, "What is the best deed?" He replied, "To believe in Allah and to fight for His Cause." I then asked, "What is the best kind of manumission [of slaves]?" He replied, "The manumission of the most expensive slave and the most beloved by his master." I said, "If I cannot afford to do that?" He said, "Help the weak or do good for a person who cannot work for himself." I said, "If I cannot do that?" He said, "Refrain from harming others, for this will be regarded as a charitable deed for your own good."

(Source: "Manumission of Slaves, Translation of Sahih Bukhari, Volume 3, Book 46, Number 694." University of Southern California USC-MSA Compendium of Muslim Texts. Available online. URL: http://www.usc.edu/dept/MSA/fundamentals/hadithsunnah/bukhari/046.sbt.html#003.046.702. Accessed March 3, 2008.)

Marriage between Arab Muslims and non-Arabs also helped speed this mixing process.

SLAVERY

The lowest class in Islamic society was slaves. Slavery was not a new practice. In fact, it had existed on the Arabian Peninsula long before Muhammad was born. In his teachings, Muhammad did not ban slavery. However, restrictions were placed on who could be enslaved and how slaves must be treated. As a result, Muhammad's teachings did improve the lives of enslaved people throughout the empire.

In the Quran, Muslims are forbidden to enslave other Muslims. They are also required to treat their slaves humanely. This included allowing slaves to marry or buy their own freedom. In addition, the Quran states that freeing one's slaves is pleasing to God and can earn forgiveness for many sins.

Muslim armies enslaved people from all the regions they conquered. Men, women, and children from Africa, Turkey, Spain, and other areas were all enslaved to work for the Islamic Empire. Slaves could be bought at any large city's slave market. The trade was very profitable throughout the empire.

There were two different types of slaves: those who worked in the home and those who served in the Islamic armies. In the eighth century, young men of Turkish origin were brought as slaves to major cities such as Baghdad to serve as palace guards. The caliphs also used enslaved Turkish soldiers as personal bodyguards.

Sometimes, slaves refused to passively accept their fate. In 869, an uprising of African slaves known as the Zanj resulted in the slaves grabbing control of Basra and other areas in southern Iraq. They turned the tables on their former masters by taking Muslims as slaves to serve them. The Zanj were able to hold onto these areas until 883.

Despite their low social standing, some slaves played an important role in the history of the empire. Through the years, the most trusted and competent slaves served not just as servants and soldiers, but also as high-ranking government officials, advisors, temporary rulers, and concubines (women who were supported by men and lived with them without being legally married to them). Concubines who had children by their masters could not be sold or given away, and they were freed when their masters died. The children of these relationships were free from birth.

One of the strongest indicators of the blurred lines between social classes occurred in the middle of the eighth century. In 744, Umayyad Yazid III became caliph. Yazid's mother, a captured Persian princess, was the slave and concubine of an earlier caliph. The last two Umayyad caliphs were also sons of slave women. And in later years, slaves actually founded dynasties. The most famous of these is the Mamluk dynasty, powerful mainly in Egypt from about 1250 to 1517.

ISLAMIC LAW

Islamic law, both moral and legal, is known as *sharia*, which may be translated as "the clear path that leads to God." All the early laws throughout the empire were taken directly from the Quran and the sunna. Sunna is the example set by Muhammad through all of his words and deeds. These words and deeds were set down in collections of writings, known as Hadith, many years after Muhammad died.

In the early days of the empire, most situations were covered by the Quran and the

The Hadith is a collection of the words and deeds of Muhammad. This beautiful edition was made in Turkey in about 1500.

Hadith. If a question arose about how a problem or conflict should be handled, the caliph and religious scholars resolved the issue by interpreting various passages in these two sources.

But as the empire expanded, Muslims came into contact with people whose cultures and customs were very different from their own. As new and unusual situations arose from this clash of cultures, situations came up that were not covered in the two holy sources. What could be done?

To solve new moral and legal questions, the Muslims developed a branch of legal study called *fiqh*. *Fiqh* involves reading and analyzing the divinely revealed sources of law, as well as applying human reason to situations that are not specifically covered in the Quran and the Hadith. People who study *fiqh* are called *fuqaha* (the singular is *faqih*).

To aid them in correctly interpreting the law, *fuqaha* looked to *ijma*—a word that means the agreement of the community. *Ijma* includes the rulings and actual practices of the faithful. In other words, *ijma* is the interpretation most commonly agreed upon by the majority of religious and legal scholars—a kind of legal precedent.

Another method of determining what is and is not lawful is *qiyas*, or reasoning based on analogy. Analogy means comparing two similar things. In law, it involves comparing new situations to similar ones in the past, and drawing conclusions from the comparison. This practice was followed by more liberal Sunni schools of law.

Toward the end of the ninth century, a number of schools of law, called *madhhabs*, developed throughout the empire. Some schools favored a stricter, more traditional way of interpreting law, using the Quran and the Hadith almost exclusively. Others favored a more liberal approach, particularly when the legal issues concerned non-religious aspects of life.

Four Sunni legal schools still exist.

CONNECTIONS

Sharia Today

In some countries where Islam dominates (or where there is a large Muslim minority), sharia is a code of conduct that is applied to the Muslim community. Nations where this is true include India, Egypt, Syria, Iraq, and Turkey.

In other countries, sharia is the law of the land. This is the case in Iran, Saudi Arabia, parts of Pakistan and Indonesia, and the northern part of Nigeria. In these countries, it is a crime to drink alcohol and for women to appear in public dressed "immodestly" (what "modesty" means in practice varies from country to country).

1. The Hanafi school, founded in southern Iraq by religious scholar Abu Hanifa (699–767), followed a more liberal tradition of using *qiyas*. In the 16th century, the Hanafi school was officially adopted by the Ottoman Turks. Today, it has the largest following of all the Sunni legal schools, and is followed in Turkey, India, and Pakistan.

2. The Hanbali school was founded in Baghdad by Ahmad ibn Hanbal (780–855). A more traditional school of law, Hanbali today is dominant on the Arabian Peninsula.

3. The Shafii school, founded by Muhammad ibn Idris al-Shafii (767–820), tried to find a middle ground between the more traditional and the more liberal interpretations of the law. This school is now followed in Southeast Asia, parts of Egypt, and parts of the Arabian Peninsula.

4. The Maliki school, founded by Malik ibn Anas (716–795), followed a more traditional method of interpreting moral and civil law, and was supported by scholars in Mecca and Medina. It was also the legal school of Islamic Spain, until its fall. Today, the Maliki school is followed in North and West Africa.

Islamic Law and Personal Conduct

Islamic law recognizes five different categories of conduct for all human actions. These categories are:

- Required or obligatory
- Recommended
- Neutral or permissible
- Reprehensible or disapproved
- Forbidden

The Five Pillars of Islam (declaration of belief, prayer, charity, fasting, and pilgrimage) are all required. Forbidden acts, also called *haram*, include eating pork, gambling, and drinking alcohol.

The Shiites and Kharijites follow their own schools of law, which have distinct differences from those of the Sunni Muslims. For example, Shiite law does not allow using *qiyas* to interpret the law. Instead, Shiite schools determine the law based directly on the Quran and the sunna.

CHAPTER 5

LIVING IN THE ISLAMIC EMPIRE

MUSLIM CONQUESTS DID NOT DESTROY THE EXISTING towns and cities. When the Muslims conquered an area, they took land only from the royals and their followers, and did not disrupt the existing system of government. The Muslims understood that to profit from their newly conquered lands, they needed to allow life to continue as before.

From the earliest days of the empire, the caliphs wanted to discourage Muslims from interacting with conquered peoples. Under Umar, the second rightly guided caliph, the Muslims began the practice of building garrison towns (towns that have soldiers permanently stationed in them) in conquered regions, where the conquerors would live apart from the conquered.

These garrison towns served several functions. First, they prevented problems from arising between Muslim troops and the newest subjects of the Islamic Empire. They also kept Muslim troops from picking up the habits and customs of the newly conquered. Finally, they made it possible for life in conquered cities and towns to continue functioning as normal, since they were not suddenly filled with Muslim soldiers.

Yet despite the measures taken to keep conquerors separate and different from the conquered, the language, religion, culture and social systems of the Arab Muslims had a profound influence on the lands they conquered. This began with Arabic, which was the official language of the empire and was required for all government business. To get along with those who held power—and to keep their jobs in the government—conquered peoples began learning to speak and write Arabic.

OPPOSITE
The first garrison town built by Caliph Umar was at Kufa. Behind the ruins of the old city rises a shrine to Ibn Aqil (1040–1119), a great Muslim religious thinker.

KUFA

The first garrison town was Kufa, in southern Iraq. It was built in 638 by General Saad, who served under Umar. Saad chose the site because it had excellent grazing lands. Here, the soldiers' camels, horses, and sheep would be well fed.

The town was built out of baked bricks and marble columns that were taken from nearby ruins. Saad's home and the mosque were in the center. Saad himself served as Kufa's governor.

In Kufa, the soldiers lived in areas of the city that were segregated by tribal associations. Within a tribal district, one clan (a group of close-knit families) might all live on one specific street. As the garrison city grew, each tribal district built its own mosques and created its own associations.

As wives and children joined the soldiers, Kufa's population skyrocketed. Just a few years after its founding, it was home to more than 40,000 people. To support this growing population, merchants soon flocked to Kufa. They expanded the city, building out from the center of the town.

Over the years, Kufa developed into one of the most important cities in the empire. It became a Shiite political center, as well as a center for learning.

BASRA

Another early garrison town in southern Iraq was Basra, founded by Umar in 635. In 665, the caliph Muawiya appointed his half-brother Ziyad commander of Basra.

Ziyad was a strict disciplinarian and ruled the town with an iron fist. He was also a brilliant administrator, implementing a registry department in Basra for official documents.

Under Ziyad's command, all official documents were sealed with wax, then marked with the governor's own peacock stamp. Ziyad even persuaded Muawiya to follow his example, marking the first time government documents were formally registered in the Islamic Empire.

BAGHDAD

Baghdad, the most glorious city built by the Muslims during the Islamic Empire, was not founded as a garrison town. In 762, the Abbasid caliph al-Mansur decided he needed a new capital for himself and his descendants. Al-Mansur wanted the new city in Iraq to serve as a symbol of the Abbasids' political, commercial, and cultural superiority.

The new capital was built on the site of an ancient Persian village that had also been named Baghdad. Mansur called his capital Madinat al-Salam, which means "City of Peace," but people continued to call it by its old name.

Baghdad was located on the west bank of the Tigris River, 20 miles northeast of the former Persian capital,

Ctesiphon. The site was wisely chosen. Because of its location between the Tigris and the Euphrates Rivers, Baghdad was surrounded by fertile land. Additionally, the city could easily be defended. Enemy troops could attack only by ship or by crossing a heavily-guarded bridge into the city.

The most skilled builders and designers from around the empire were brought to Baghdad to work on the royal complex. About 100,000 men worked four years to complete the Abbasid city.

Baghdad originally was known as the Round City. It was built in a circular plan and measured nearly 2 miles across. The city was made up of three circles set inside one another, each one surrounded by a wall. The caliph's palace and the mosque were built in the innermost circle. In the middle circle lived courtiers, army officers, and other important people. The third circle was occupied by the rest of the people.

The outermost wall was a strong one, with four gates leading to the four different points of the empire. Each gate was defended by a company of 1,000 soldiers. Merchants and businessmen set up their shops outside the outermost wall.

The city continued to grow and spread. By the early 800s, Baghdad was the largest city in the Middle East. At its height, more than 1 million people made their homes there. During the reign of Caliph Harun al-Rashid (r. 786–809), Baghdad expanded to the east side of the Tigris River, and this area soon became the heart of the city.

During the Abbasid dynasty, Baghdad became the most important trading city in the empire. It has remained a vibrant and important place through the centuries. The Haydar Khana mosque in Baghdad was built in 1836.

At its best, the city was the most cultured, beautiful, and busy metropolitan area in the world. It contained breathtaking mosques, palaces, and gardens. Like other cities throughout the empire, Baghdad was home to libraries, colleges, and hospitals. The busy boat traffic on the Tigris made it an avenue of trade. Gondolas (small, flat-bottomed boats) sailed up and down, filled with goods and people.

Because it was located in the heart of the former Sassanian Empire, Baghdad's residents and visitors could not help but be influenced by Persian culture. As a result, a Persian influence began to spread throughout the empire.

In addition to the Persian influence, the city enjoyed a truly international atmosphere. As capital of the huge Islamic Empire, Baghdad attracted people from all over the world to study and do business. Scholars, poets, scientists, and other learned people came to visit and study at the libraries, mosques, and schools. Caliph Harun al-Rashid had a library with close to 600,000 books.

Baghdad continued to be one of the most cultured and beautiful cities in the world until 1258, when it was destroyed and looted by the Mongols. The destruction marked the end of the Islamic Empire.

CAIRO

Another center of Islamic culture was Cairo in Egypt. Cairo, located on the banks of the Nile River, was founded in 969 by the Fatimids. It served as a center of government, culture, and commerce throughout the Fatimid dynasty.

From Cairo, the Fatimids took control of the gold mines of Nubia, along the upper Nile. With Nubian gold, the Fatimids controlled one of the richest regions in the empire. The gold enabled them to pay huge armies, buy supplies, and send out missionaries to convert people to Islam.

The Nile River was the center of life in Cairo, and was treated with reverence and care. It was important to maintaining the waterways and irrigation canals that watered the area's crops, and the caliph appointed several officials to make sure these things were done. The Nile also served as the means for transporting goods, people, and communications to other points in the Islamic Empire. The river made Cairo a center of the trade between the Mediterranean region and India.

Close to Cairo was its twin city, Fustat, a garrison town founded around 641 by Muslims. Fustat was another important and thriving Egyptian town. The two cities eventually merged.

CORDOBA

Cordoba in southern Spain has a long history of being influenced by conquerors. The city was founded around the first century B.C.E. by the Romans. In 572, it was taken from the Romans by the Visigoths, a Germanic tribe. The Muslims took it from the Visigoths in 711. In 756, Abd al-Rahman, the Umayyad prince who had escaped being slaughtered by the Abbasids, took control of Cordoba.

As the capital of the Umayyad emirs in Spain, Cordoba became the jewel of Europe. It was also a center of trade and industry in the area, and the city grew rich and prospered. It was famous for the production of silk and paper. Cordoban craftsmen were especially admired for a deep red decorated leather that they produced. It came to be known—and is still known today—as cordovan.

Cordoba was also a center of learning and culture, not only for the Muslim world but for Europe as well. From Cordoba and other cities in Spain, poetry, science, philosophy, and medical knowledge was absorbed from the eastern Islamic Empire and spread into Europe. Scholars in Cordoba directly influenced European scholars, including such writers as Thomas Aquinas (1225–1274) and Dante Alighieri (1265–1321).

By the early 900s, Cordoba was the largest city on the Iberian Peninsula, with as many as 500,000 people living there. Even Muslims from other parts of the empire believed Cordoba was one of the most beautiful cities in the Muslim world. Many who visited the city chose to move and make their homes there.

CONNECTIONS

"Moorish" Architecture

The influence of the Islamic conquerors on architectural styles can still be seen today in areas that were once part of the Islamic Empire, especially in southern Spain. What became known as "Moorish" architecture made its way to the Americas with the earliest Spanish explorers. These explorers built houses, missions, and other buildings that reminded them of their homes back in Spain.

In the United States, the influence of Islamic architecture is especially strong in the Southwest. Here, Moorish touches can be seen in buildings that were built hundreds of years ago, as well as those built more recently. These touches include horseshoe-shaped archways, red-tiled roofs, smooth stucco outer walls, ceramic tiles, heavy wooden doors, and courtyards with a central fountain surrounded by arcades.

The so-called Mediterranean Revival style of building that was popular in Florida in the early 1900s includes elements of Moorish, Spanish, Italian, Venetian, and other styles. Today, home builders can choose a "Spanish" type of home that incorporates some Moorish features into its design.

Rosary Beads

Rosary beads, strings of beads used by Roman Catholics to count prayers, were borrowed by the Spanish St. Dominic (ca. 1170–1221) from an Islamic practice. Muslims use a chain of 99 beads to count off the 99 different names of God.

Cordoba remained under Muslim control until 1236, when it was conquered by Ferdinand of Castile (1199–1252), the king of Spain.

TRADE AND INDUSTRY

From the earliest days of the empire, trade was the most important industry. Early Muslim merchants were responsible for the wealth and prosperity of the empire. They also helped spread Islam, Arabic, and Arabian-Islamic culture. Kharijite merchants in North Africa, for example, helped spread their particular brand of Islam to the people there. As a result, the Kharijites are strongest in this area today.

At first, trade throughout the empire was primarily over land. Caravans of camels loaded with goods from India, Southeast Asia, and China trekked across the desert. They carried such items as grain, silk, cloth, wines, dried fruits, ivory, wood, perfume, and precious gems and metals. Trade with Africa for gold and slaves was also an important part of the merchant industry.

Western Europe was of little importance as a trading partner. According to historian Bernard Lewis in *The Muslim Discovery of Europe*, exports from Europe were "too few and too insignificant" to deserve mention during the empire's earliest days.

The caravans traveled slowly, usually at about 3 miles an hour. At various points along the route, they could stop at a *caravanserai*, a sort of crude motel. Here, the caravan leader would find a room for himself and a place for his camels to rest, eat, and drink.

Caravans faced many obstacles. Perhaps the most serious was the hot, dry desert. Bandits were also common along some caravan routes. But merchants were quite willing to face the risks because of the huge profits involved. The wealthiest people in the early Islamic Empire were those who had successful trading businesses.

As the empire expanded, the demand for exotic goods from remote corners of the empire also grew. In addition, people in large cities such as Baghdad required constant supplies of food and other trade items. With so much demand, land trade was soon supplemented with trade by ship.

Merchant ships traveled from port to port, transporting goods more efficiently and easily throughout the huge area of the Muslim Empire. Muslim traders may have operated as far north as the Baltic region and northern Europe.

ﭐﻟﻘﺮﺁﻥ ﺛﻢ ﺯﺍﺑﻌﻞ ﺃﺳﺎﻃﻴﺮ ﺑﻼ ﻣﺎ ﻭﺯﺧﺎﺭﻑ ﺟﻠﺎ ﻣﺎ ﻭﻗﺎﻝ ﺃﺯﻛﺒﻮﺍ ﻓﻴﻬﺎ ﺑﺴﻢ ﺍﻟﻠﻪ ﻣﺠﺮﺍﻫﺎ
ﻭﻣﺮﺳﺎﻫﺎﺕ ﺛﻢ ﻣﻦ ﻳﻨﻘﻞ ﺍﻟﻤﻌﻤﻴﻦ ﺃﻭ ﻋﺒﺎﺩ ﺍﻟﻠﻪ ﺍﻟﻤﻜﺮﻣﻴﻦ ﻗﺎﻝ ﻟﻬﺎ ﺃﻧﺎ

Trade was the most important industry in the Islamic Empire. Merchant ships traveled from port to port. This is a 13th-century illustration.

The Islamic Empire had many important port cities. One key port was Siraf, located on the eastern coast of the Persian Gulf. Foods from Oman and goods from Africa, India, and other areas arrived by *dhows*, small boats with triangular sails, called lateen sails. The goods were then transported by camel caravans to other parts of the empire.

During the Abbasid dynasty, Baghdad quickly became the most important trading city. Goods from all over the empire were shipped up the Tigris River. At the markets of Baghdad, people could buy exotic foods and unusual trinkets. Here they might find porcelain, silk, and paper from China; gemstones from central Asia; and furs from Scandinavia. Baghdad was also an export center, with the empire's goods shipped out to lands far and wide.

CONNECTIONS

Check, Please

Banking and commerce in the Islamic Empire was more complex and advanced than anything in Europe at the time. In fact, it would take about three centuries for the Europeans to catch up.

A number of Islamic banking concepts are still used in the financial world today. For example, people throughout the empire understood the concept of credit. They wrote up special documents that could be cashed at a bank or any of its branches throughout the empire. These documents were called *sakk*, from which we get the word *check*.

Other Islamic contributions live on in words that we now use to describe commercial and financial ideas. For example, the word *average* comes from the Arabic word *awariyah*, meaning damaged goods. By the 17th century, the word had evolved to mean the fair distribution of losses due to damaged goods.

Another Arabic word still used in the business world is *tariff*, which is a tax on imported goods. During the Islamic Empire, tariffs were announcements or notifications that were posted so that merchants knew how much tax to pay the empire on shipments of imported goods.

The word *carat*, which we use to describe the weight of precious metals and stones, comes from the Arabic word *qirat*. To merchants throughout the empire, *qirat* was a measure equal to one seed from a carob tree, or four grains. The seeds were used to balance a scale when weighing out gold.

As trade developed, there was a need for a standard system of money and common banking practices. During the Abbasid dynasty, two types of currency were used: In the eastern part of the empire, the Persian silver *dirham* was the standard unit of money. The Byzantine gold *denarius* was used in the west. The values of these two currencies went up and down relative to one another, just as the value of currency does today.

To handle currency exchanges, money changers became common in markets across the empire. As the money changer began lending funds and offering credit, his role developed into that of a banker. Because the Quran forbids Muslims from lending money with interest, early bankers in the empire were usually Jewish or Christian. Often they operated with Muslim merchants as partners.

Textile production was a major Islamic industry. Cities around the empire produced cloth made of silk, linen, cotton, flax, and wool. One special type of textile made in the empire was *tiraz*, which was cotton or linen cloth embroidered with passages from the Quran. The cloth was made in special workshops, also called *tiraz*, which were controlled by the caliph. Every piece made included the name and location of the workshop, the date, and the name of the current caliph.

Conquests and border wars made the business of war a profitable one. Cordoba, for example, was home to workshops that manufactured thousands of tents, shields, bows, and arrows each year to supply the Islamic armies. Horses and camels to carry soldier's goods were also bred and sold.

Craftsmen throughout the empire shared their skills with one another, and the technology of one area soon spread to another. Artisans from Baghdad, for example, went to Spain and North Africa to share their metal working techniques. From there, such skills as metalworking, weaving, and leather tanning were eventually transmitted throughout Europe.

FOOD IN THE EMPIRE

From the eighth century to the 13th century, most subjects of the Islamic Empire enjoyed a good life, thanks to the wealth of the vast empire. Although early Arabs, particularly Bedouin tribes, generally lived on dates, milk, and the occasional bit of meat, this was no longer the case as the Muslims conquered new lands. As the empire expanded, Muslims were exposed to many exotic foods and their diets became quite varied.

Cookbooks from the Islamic Empire still survive today, giving historians a glimpse into what its subjects ate. The first cookbook written in Arabic was compiled by Ibrahim ibn al-Mahdi (779–839), uncle of the caliph al-Mamun (r. 813–833).

IN THEIR OWN WORDS

An Islamic Cookbook

This is from a collection of recipes written down in the 13th century in Spain. At the time, southern Spain was part of the Islamic Empire.

UJJA *(FRITTATA) OF PIGEONS*

Take two clean, active pigeons, and fry them in a pan with fresh oil; then place them in a pot and add to them some murri naqî, vinegar, oil, cilantro, Chinese cinnamon and thyme; when it is cooked, break eight eggs with it and pour out. It is finished.

Murri naqî is spices mixed with honey, water, lemon, and bread and then cooked. It is one of a group of condiments that were popular in early Islamic cooking and that vanished some time after the 14th century.

(Source: "An Anonymous Andalusian Cookbook of the 13th Century," translated by Charles Perry. Recreational Medievalism. Available online. URL: http://www.davidd friedman.com/Medieval/Cookbooks/Andalusian/ andalusian1.htm#Heading6. Accessed March 6, 2008.)

The book contained recipes for many gourmet dishes that were served to the caliph and the rest of the court. These include a pureed eggplant and walnut dish and baked hen served on top of flatbread.

Muslims could buy all kinds of foods at the local outdoor market. One type of shop, called a *harras*, sold ground meat that was combined with wheat and then fried. Other shops sold sauces, relishes, breads, and desserts.

Eggplant was probably the most common vegetable. It was used in a variety of dishes and could be prepared in many different ways. Lentils were also popular. However, only the wealthiest subjects ate meats such as lamb, chicken, or veal. Pork was not eaten, because Muslim dietary law forbids it.

Spices were an important part of the preparation of any meal. Popular cooking spices included cardamom, ginger, turmeric, and coriander. These spices gave Middle Eastern cuisine the distinct flavor it retains to this day. The Arabs introduced these spices to Europe.

Water was the drink of choice. Because of their desert history, many Muslims considered water to be a source of life and purification. To give a person water, according to Muhammad, was an act that deserved the highest praise.

The Muslims did enjoy other drinks, though. One was *sekanjabin*, which was water flavored with mint syrup. Water was also flavored with lemons, violets, roses, bananas, and many other sweet substances. Drinking alcoholic beverages was forbidden.

Despite the variety of foods available, dates retained their popularity and importance. These

CONNECTIONS

Islamic Cuisine

Many people have heard the story that Italian merchant Marco Polo (1254–1324) introduced pasta to Europe in 1298 after he returned from China. Several historians, however, believe that pasta was introduced into Italy centuries earlier—by Muslim invaders in Sicily. The first pasta—balls and strings of dried flour—may have been invented by Arab conquerors in their search to find a food that could be easily transported from battle to battle.

Another important food contribution was sugar cane. This popular sweetener first came to Europe from the Islamic Empire, and it was one of the top commodities traded until the 18th century. With the introduction of sugar cane to Europe, sweets of all sorts quickly became popular. The words *candy, caramel, marzipan, sherbet, sugar,* and *syrup* are all Arabic in origin.

Other culinary contributions that we still eat today include flat breads, which were popular and eaten with most meals. In the United States, these flat breads take the form of pita and wraps. Other Middle Eastern foods that made their way to Europe and other parts of the world include falafel (ground chickpeas and spices that are shaped into balls and fried) and hummus, a kind of dip also made with chickpeas and spices.

sweet, fleshy fruits from the date palm tree were served fresh or used to make other desserts. Dates were even used to make a type of alcoholic beverage called *khamr*, which was popular despite the Islamic prohibition on drinking alcohol.

Before a meal was served, it was important for all guests to wash their hands. A pitcher of water and a basin were always located near the table for this purpose. During the Abbasid dynasty, food was brought out on big brass trays and set on a low table. Diners used their thumb and the first two fingers of their right hand to eat. It was considered bad manners to lick one's fingers.

CONNECTIONS

Dietary Restrictions

Muslims today must follow the same dietary laws that Muslims in the Islamic Empire followed. One such law forbids Muslims the eating of pork. In addition, all meat must be slaughtered following specific rituals passed down through the centuries. This type of meat is called halal, which means "allowed" or "permitted" in Arabic. Most large U.S. cities today have halal butchers where Muslims can buy meat that has been prepared properly and has not come into contact with non-halal meat.

HOMES AND WHAT WAS IN THEM

The expansion of the empire brought a change of lifestyle for many Arabs. Although many Bedouins chose to continue living their nomadic desert lifestyle, others built permanent homes in the newly-conquered lands.

For the wealthy, the home consisted of a large single building with a central open courtyard. The courtyard often had a fountain or a garden in the center. In many cases, extended families lived together in these big houses, with different branches of the family living in separate apartments.

Inside, the apartments contained little furniture. Ornate rugs or cushions were thrown over small square mattresses for the family to sit on.

Floor coverings were important to Muslims. Rugs were both practical and decorative. They served as places for prayer, rest, eating, and entertaining. In mosques, at home, or as decorations for a royal palace, carpets were highly prized. The caliph Harun al-Rashid had 22,000 rugs in his palace.

Even before Islam, carpets were important and multi-functional belongings. They were used not only as cushions, blankets, and pillows

Rugs were important in many Eastern cultures, even before and after the Islamic Empire. This silk rug was made in the 17th century in India, at a time when India was ruled by the Mughals—Muslim descendants of the Mongols. The picture represents the Muslim image of paradise, with Muhammad at the center. The faces of the figures are not shown, because Islam discourages the depiction of specific people in artwork.

when a nomad was at home in his tent, but were also useful during travel. Rugs could be thrown across the back of a camel or horse like a saddle, or used as sacks to carry possessions.

Some rugs were huge works of art that took months, even years, to create. They might include distinctive ornamental patterns such as outlines of flowers, leaves, fruit or geometric patterns (collectively known today as arabesque, which means "in the manner of Arabs"). These pictures were created by the careful placement and tying of thousands of knots. Pictures of gardens were also popular. Particularly spectacular rugs might also be hung on the walls. Rugs were made of every fiber from wool to silk. Some were even woven with silver and gold thread and studded with gemstones.

One common use for rugs was in prayer. Prayer rugs, large enough for one person to kneel on, could be carried to and from the mosque or laid down wherever the person was, making it easier to kneel in worship. Prayer rugs often had a mihrab (niche in a mosque indicating the direction of Mecca) woven into them, with a rectangle above that the worshipper could touch his forehead to. Other decorations might include items commonly found in the mosque, such as hanging lanterns, archways, and verses from the Quran.

Painted and decorated tiles, an art borrowed from the Byzantine Empire, were popular and often graced floors and walls. Decorated tiles were especially popular with the Seljuk Turks. They were used to cover walls, ceilings, and floors in mosques, bath houses, private homes, and royal palaces.

CONNECTIONS

The Mattress Comes to Europe

One of the new ideas brought back to Europe by crusaders was the mattress. The crusaders borrowed the Arabic practice of sleeping on pillows, cushions, and rugs thrown upon the floor. Before that, the common people in Europe slept on piles of straw, tree boughs, or similar material heaped in a corner of their house. The word *mattress* comes from the Arabic word *matrah*, which means a place where something is thrown.

During the later Abbasid dynasty, the *diwan*, a sofa that stretched along three sides of the room, became popular. Today, another word for sofa is divan, which specifically means a long, backless sofa with pillows, set against a wall.

STYLE

The early Bedouin people wore simple clothes designed to protect themselves from the scorching rays of the desert sun. Their clothing consisted of a long shirt with a sash (*sash* is an Arabic word) and a flowing upper garment.

As the empire expanded, the basic style of clothing remained the same, with some refinements. Women and men alike continued to wear long shirts that covered the upper part of the body. Beneath this tunic they wore loose pants. Women covered their heads with long, flowing scarves and veils, while men often wore cloaks around their shoulders. These cloaks were multi-functional, serving as a rain or sun shield, a blanket, or a sack to carry goods.

Muslim men, like women, also covered their heads. Many used pieces of cloth that could be wrapped around the head in many different ways, similar to today's turban.

The courtiers of the Abbasid dynasty introduced many new styles to the empire. During warmer weather, silk gowns became the fashion. In colder weather, quilted clothing was popular.

Muslim men at court often dyed their beards with henna to redden them. This was a custom that dated back to the time of Muhammad. They also trimmed their hair short to reveal their necks and ears.

Cosmetics were used in the court of the Abbasid caliphs. Women used black kohl under their eyes to accentuate the size of their eyes. They also dyed their fingertips with henna to redden them. Perfumes were popular too, for men and women. Men, for example, sometimes scented their beards before dining. Rosewater was a favorite scent.

The Abbasid caliphs' wives often set fashion trends that were followed by Muslim women. One wife decorated her shoes with gemstones—a fashion that has endured to this day. Another, to cover a blemish on her forehead, designed a jeweled, lacy veil that quickly became the latest rage among Baghdad women. Abbasid women also wore anklets, bracelets, and other pieces of jewelry.

Cleanliness was extremely important to the people of the Islamic Empire. While people in Europe believed that bathing was dangerous and unhealthy, the people of the empire believed in rubbing the body with pleasant-smelling lotions, cleaning the teeth with a stick and paste, and using perfumes to mask foul body and other odors.

Public baths were particularly popular, especially during the Abbasid dynasty. Baghdad alone had thousands of them. The baths had hot and cold running water. The hot water was heated by huge fireplaces. Bathers used ground ashes as soap.

The public baths provided social opportunities, giving men the chance to relax with other men. They also gave women one of their rare opportunities to get out of the house and socialize with other women.

WOMEN AND FAMILY LIFE

Throughout the Islamic Empire, marriage was considered a sacred institution and, for men, a duty. Men usually married for the first time around the age of 20, while women were sometimes as young as 12. Families generally arranged the marriages, with the husband's family giving the bride a dowry (property or money brought by a bride or groom to their marriage), which was hers to keep.

According to the Quran, men were allowed to have up to four wives, while women could have just one husband. However, the husband had to treat each wife equally and be able to take care of all of his

Keeping Clean in the Islamic Empire

For the Arab people, personal cleanliness was always important. During the height of the Islamic Empire, the Arabs were the first to use hard soap made out of olive oil, alkali, and natron, a type of salt. Under Muslim control, Italy and Spain became soap-making centers. From here, soap was exported to other parts of Europe.

Muslims in Spain and Italy also helped popularize the connection between cleanliness and health. Muslim doctors put forth many theories about the role that poor hygiene played in sickness and the spread of disease.

Hammamat, or bathhouses, were believed to play a key role in preventing contagious diseases from spreading. They were even known as "silent doctors." Inspectors carefully examined each *hammam* to make sure it was kept clean. Today, *hammamat* are still found throughout the Middle East. Many are attached to mosques.

The Muslims also popularized dental hygiene. Although they did not invent the toothbrush or toothpaste, Muslim doctors helped advance knowledge of the mouth and teeth, and the need to keep them clean.

wives financially. This meant providing each wife with her own cooking and sleeping areas, and her own slaves. Most Muslim men had just one wife at a time.

After the death of Khadija, Muhammad himself practiced polygamy—having more than one wife. He was allowed as many wives as he liked, and at one time had nine wives. Although he married most of his wives for political reasons, he also married for love.

Muhammad was the first Muslim to create a harem, or restricted place, for his wives. The wives were separated from other people so that they could not be held to blame for any behavior that might be considered improper.

Each wife lived in her own small apartment. When male visitors came to the house, a curtain called the *hijab* was put up to prevent them from seeing Muhammad's wives. But the *hijab* gradually came to mean more than a curtain. Eventually it became the custom of Muslim women wearing a veil, head covering, and modest dress in public, including covering their arms and legs. *Hijab*, meaning modest attire, is still worn by many Muslim women today. The word *hijab* also refers to the veil and head covering itself.

This painting of a man preaching in the mosque shows the women and children separated from the main room.

The Quran made other important changes in the life of Arab women. They could now keep their dowries even if their husband divorced them. The Quran also stipulated that a man must treat his wife kindly. Islamic law also allowed women to inherit and own property, separate from male family members.

The first duty of women throughout the empire was to care for the home and their families. At home, some women had their own small businesses, especially spinning or dyeing cloth. Because they were supposed to stay at home and could not bring their goods to the marketplace, they had to hire men to sell their goods on their behalf.

Poorer women probably had more freedom of movement, because wealthier Arab men tended to keep their wives home and out of sight. These wealthy women had slaves who took care of their household chores for them, but the poor did not have this luxury. Wealthier women seem to have been covered up more in their clothing than the poor, as well.

However, as has been the case throughout history, the financial resources of wealthier women certainly gave them more options. They could have servants, could give away property, and had more private space. In some cases, they were able to attend school and take up a profession. Some wealthy Muslim women, for example, practiced medicine and operated as merchants.

Men were under no restrictions to remain at home. For entertainment, they could go to the public baths, play chess with their friends, or hang out at the local tavern. Although alcohol was forbidden, taverns served a fermented liquid called *nabidh*, made from raisins or dates.

At the tavern, the men might be entertained by music or

IN THEIR OWN WORDS

The Clever Courtier

How could a courtier stay out of trouble? According to vizier Nizam al-Mulk (d. 1092), the perfect courtier should always agree with everything the caliph had to say and:

[S]hould be essentially honorable and of excellent character, of cheerful disposition and irreproachable in respect of his religion, discreet and a clean liver. He should be able to tell a story and repeat a narrative either humorous or grave, and he should remember news. He should also be consistently a carrier of pleasant tidings and the announcer of felicitous [fortunate] happenings. He should also have acquaintance of backgammon and chess, and if he can play a musical instrument and can handle a weapon, it is all the better.

(Source: Nizam al-Mulk. "On the Courtiers and Familiars of Kings," from *Treatise on the Art of Government*, translated by Reuben Levy, M.A., 1929. Medieval Sourcebook. Available online. URL: http://www.fordham.edu/halsall/source/nizam-courtiers.html. Accessed September 18, 2009.)

CONNECTIONS

Salukis: The Dogs of Caliphs

The Saluki is one of the oldest-known breeds of domesticated dogs. Thousands of years ago, Bedouin tribes used the sharp-eyed and lightning-fast Salukis, also known as gazelle hounds, to hunt gazelle and other animals. The dogs were so highly prized that they were even allowed to sleep in the tents of their masters.

In ancient Egypt, the dogs were kept by pharaohs and became known as the "royal dogs of Egypt." Only royalty were allowed to keep these animals, and a favorite dog might be mummified and placed in his master's tomb.

After the rise of the Islamic Empire, the dogs became popular as the pets of the caliphs. They accompanied the caliph on hunting expeditions, and were often given to friends and important people as signs of royal favor and esteem.

Salukis are sleek, silky animals that hunt by sight and are part of a group of dogs known as sighthounds. Like Greyhounds, they are swift and intelligent animals. In some countries, Salukis are raced against one another.

poetry recitations. However, at home there were restrictions on with whom men could socialize (particularly in the homes of non-relatives). Women usually had more freedom than men to socialize in private homes.

For children, education began at home. From an early age, children were taught to memorize passages from the Quran. As they grew older, the Quran and the Hadith were used to teach them to read. Later, boys would receive more formal lessons at mosques, schools, or Islamic centers.

During the Abbasid dynasty, boys usually began attending mosque schools at around the age of seven—as long as their families could afford to pay a small tuition.

Wealthier boys continued their education longer. They might attend seminars, discuss poetry, and read classic works of Greek that had been translated into Arabic. These lessons prepared the wealthy young men for positions of importance. The empire's first universities were founded in the 10th century under the Abbasid dynasty.

Two Abbasid caliphs, al-Mahdi and al-Hadi, were responsible for the construction of a large number of libraries and centers of education in Baghdad. Scientists and scholars from all over the empire went to the capital to teach and learn in the universities (also known as "houses of knowledge") and madrasas (Islamic schools).

IT IS GOOD TO BE THE CALIPH

The ruling dynasty—especially the Abbasids—lived a much different life than did the average Muslim in the Islamic Empire. As the Abbasid caliphs passed their control over the government to others, they turned to a life of rituals, pleasure, and entertainment.

The caliph was almost constantly surrounded by courtiers. Those who wished to meet with the caliph had to kneel down in front of the ruler and kiss the floor. During the early Abbasid dynasty, a leather carpet was kept unrolled before the caliph's throne. If need be, the royal executioner could step up, chop off the head of anyone who displeased the caliph, then take the dead body away without making a mess. The executioner was always ready, with his sword drawn, to obey the caliph's signal.

The Abbasids enjoyed many different types of entertainment. Musicians and poets were very popular at court, and the most talented ones often received regular payments from the caliph. Another popular pastime was hunting. The caliph rode on horseback, using dogs, falcons, ferrets, and even cheetahs to help him track wild game.

As might be expected, dining was a grand experience at the palace. Under the caliph al-Mamun, diners were offered foods from far away that were shipped in lead boxes packed with snow to keep them fresh. Al-Mamun's guests were also the first Arabs to dine using tables and chairs instead of sitting on the floor. The caliph's tables were made of gold and silver.

Harems became more common during the Abbasid dynasty. In addition to their four wives allowed by the Quran, caliphs kept hundreds—sometimes thousands—of concubines. Concubines might be female slaves or prisoners of war who caught the caliph's eye. Eunuchs (castrated slaves) were often employed to guard the women.

HOLIDAYS

Throughout the empire, Muslims observed several religious and nonreligious celebrations. The most important religious holiday throughout the kingdom was Eid al-Adha (the feast of sacrifice). The holiday

CONNECTIONS

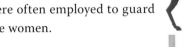

Fun and Games

Chess was the caliph's game of choice. He even held chess championships at the palace. While this game of strategy had come to Persia from India, it was introduced to Europe by the Muslims. The term *checkmate*, which in chess means one player has cornered the other's king, comes from the Arabic phrase *shah mat*, which means "the king is dead."

Other games borrowed from the Persians and popularized by the Muslims include polo and backgammon—both of which are still played today.

marked the end of the sacred pilgrimage to Mecca. On the 10th day of Dhu al-Hijja (the final month of the Islamic calendar), an animal was sacrificed and prayers were offered. During the rest of the four-day holiday, Muslims feasted and visited family.

Another major religious holiday, Eid al-Fitr (the feast of breaking fast), marked the end of the fast of Ramadan. (A fast is a period in which one does not eat.) Under the Abbasid dynasty, long processions were organized, followed by a huge feast that might last up to three days. At the feast, diners ate such specially-prepared dishes as thin pancakes, breads, and dried fruits. On the streets of Baghdad, subjects were entertained by musicians and poets.

One secular (nonreligious) holiday enjoyed by the Fatimids in North Africa was Nawruz, a festival that had its roots in ancient Iran. During Nawruz, some Muslims celebrated the return of spring. The celebration included dancing, bonfires, and giving gifts to friends and family. It was also customary to give a gift to the caliph. However, some religious scholars felt that good Muslims should not celebrate this holiday, because of its secular roots.

This 13th-century illustration shows a Muslim man being buried. Most Muslim graves were simple and people were often buried without a coffin.

DEATH AND BURIAL

The Quran offers Muslims hope of an afterlife. According to Islam, the soul, freed from the body, moves on to a new phase. Those who have lived a righteous life are rewarded with heaven, while those who have not are sent to hell.

When a Muslim died, the body was first washed to purify it. Then it was wrapped in a seamless white cloth called a shroud. Cloth for funeral shrouds had been dipped into the waters of Mecca's sacred Zamzam well during a pilgrimage.

Throughout these preparations, passages from the Quran were recited

The Zamzam Well

The Zamzam well is located in Mecca, a few yards east of the Kaaba. It is 115 feet deep and is topped by an elegant dome.

Muslims believe that Allah created the well to provide for Hagar, a wife of the Biblical figure Abraham (the Judeo-Christian Bible says Hagar was a servant in Abraham's household), who was the mother of Ishmael. When Hagar was forced to leave Abraham's household, she and her baby son wandered in the desert and eventually were overcome with thirst. In her desperate search for water, Hagar ran seven times back and forth between the two hills of Safa and Marwa. Then, in despair, she sat down and waited to die. Allah saw her effort and miraculously blessed the spot with a spring.

Muslims on the hajj pilgrimage recall this event by circling the same hills seven times, and by drinking the water of the Zamzam well. It is said to be able to satisfy both thirst and hunger. Pilgrims to Mecca collect the water in bottles to bring home to relatives and friends who are ill, because it is also said to have healing powers.

over the body. Finally, the body was buried on its side, facing Mecca. Martyrs—those who had died advancing the cause of Islam—were to be buried as they died, with no washing or other preparation.

All Muslims had to be buried the morning after their death. During the burial, women—sometimes paid professional mourners—cried out in grief for the dead person. Mourners wore bands of cloth around their head as a symbol of their grief.

Because Muhammad opposed fancy memorials to the dead, most Muslim graves were simple and plain. People were often buried without a coffin. However, wealthy Muslims were often buried in large, domed tombs.

The last words spoken at the grave during burial were also the first words a Muslim heard as an infant: "There is no God but Allah, and Muhammad is His Prophet."

CHAPTER 6

ISLAMIC ART, SCIENCE, AND CULTURE

THE ISLAMIC EMPIRE WAS THE MOST ADVANCED civilization of its time. Much of what historians think of as Islamic culture did not come from the Arabs, though. Learning, science, and customs were all influenced by the people the Muslims conquered. Jews, Christians, and Hindus, Greeks, Persians, and Africans all contributed to the development of what we know as Islamic culture. As the empire grew, the conquerors incorporated new elements into their own civilization, often improving on the originals.

There were, of course, two major Arab contributions to Islamic culture: the Muslim religion and the Arabic language. Arabic was the language of the conquerors, and so it became the language of government and learning. It replaced Persian, Greek, and many other languages throughout the empire. Conquered people who wanted to succeed under their new rulers quickly learned Arabic. As a result, Arabic served as a powerful cultural unifier.

Islamic culture first blossomed during the Umayyad dynasty. The Umayyads were heavily influenced by Arab traditions, as well as by the Byzantines. The empire's true golden age, however, came during the Abbasid dynasty. The years 786 to 809, under Caliph Harun al-Rashid, were especially fruitful. Muslim cities became centers of world culture.

Scholars throughout the empire learned about science and philosophy by reading the works of the ancient Greeks. But ancient Greek itself was not a widely known language. The first people to translate Greek works were mainly Jews and Christians in Syria. The works of the philosophers Aristotle (384–322 B.C.E.) and Plato (ca. 429–347 B.C.E.), the mathematician Euclid (flourished in the 300s B.C.E.), and the doctors

OPPOSITE
Islamic calligraphers turned the pages of the Quran into works of art. In fact, illustrating the Quran was considered to be a kind of worship. This 14th-century manuscript is from Persia.

Galen (ca. 129–200 B.C.E.) and Hippocrates (ca. 460–377 B.C.E.), were all translated into Syriac (the language of Syria) and then into Arabic.

These Arabic translations of the Greek masters were preserved in vast libraries throughout the Islamic Empire. Thanks to them, Europe was eventually exposed to these important works of mathematics, astronomy, and logic.

Not all of the Greeks were considered worthy of translation, however. The works of playwrights and poets, including Homer (before 700 B.C.E.) and Sophocles (ca. 496–406 B.C.E.), were not considered practical or important. They were not translated, and a few centuries had to pass before their work was rediscovered.

SACRED TEXTS

Before the empire, the peoples of Arabia relied mainly on oral tradition (memorizing and reciting long works) to preserve their literature and history. But as the empire grew, great works of literature were written down. The most famous is the Quran, the sacred text of Islam. There were also other important pieces composed during the six centuries of the empire, including beautiful poetry and humorous prose. Literature composed throughout the history of the empire continues to be read and appreciated today.

The Quran is the most important and earliest piece of Arabic prose writing (although it also has some poetic elements). For Muslims, the book is more than just a piece of literature—it is a way of life.

The Quran is the written record of the messages Muhammad received directly from God. The messages were not written down by Muhammad, however, but were written after his death by people who had heard him reciting and explaining God's word. The most important message of the Quran is that there is only one God.

The holy book is written in Arabic. It is divided into 114 chapters called suras. Except for the first one, which is a prayer to God, the suras are ordered from longest to shortest. No one could be sure about the order in which Muhammad received these messages from God, so they were arranged by length.

In the early 650s, during the reign of Caliph Uthman, a standard edition of the Quran was approved. Many historians consider this to be Uthman's main achievement. He ordered all other versions of the Quran to be destroyed, although some were not.

Second in importance to the Quran is the Hadith. The Hadith, which means "narrative," is a collection of the sayings and deeds of Muhammad, compiled almost two centuries after his death. The sunna, or tradition of Muhammad's teachings, speeches, and actions, is based on the Hadith and the Hadith is an important reference for how good Muslims should think and act. Sunni Muslims recognize six collections of Hadith, which together include thousands of reports (the individual reports are also called *hadiths*).

After the death of Muhammad in 632, stories of his words and deeds were passed down orally from person to person. Beginning in the late eighth century, religious scholars began trying to confirm the accuracy of the various collections of Hadith by researching the chain of people who had told each story. As the scholars researched the roots of each story, they weeded out tales that could not be traced to trustworthy tellers. To prove its authenticity, each *hadith* begins with an *isnad*, which is a list of the people who transmitted the tale. The ideal *hadith* can be traced back to a family member or companion of Muhammad.

The first *hadiths* were written down in the late 800s. This collection has guided Islamic politics, religion, and law ever since.

POETRY

People of the Arabian Peninsula had a love for the spoken word. A Bedouin proverb (quoted by Philip K. Hitti in the book *The Arabs: A Short History*) says, "The beauty of man lies in the eloquence of his tongue." In each tribe, tales were told that had been memorized and handed down from generation to generation. These stories celebrated the bravery of the tribe, related tales of its heroes, and ridiculed its enemies. Each clan had its own poet who was the storehouse of tribal history and legends, and also often acted as the clan's spokesman. Before Islam, poetry contests in Mecca pitted the clans' chief poets against one another.

Some of the best poems, both long and short, were hung on the walls of the Kaaba, where Muhammad allowed them to remain after he returned to Mecca. Today, these poems are known as the Hanged Poems. The overall structure of the poem was considered less important than the craftsmanship of each individual line, and each line is a work of art in itself. As a result, these poems are sometimes called "strings of pearls."

The Poem of Zuhair is one of the Hanged Poems. The poem is long, and each line is able to stand on its own without the rest of the poem.

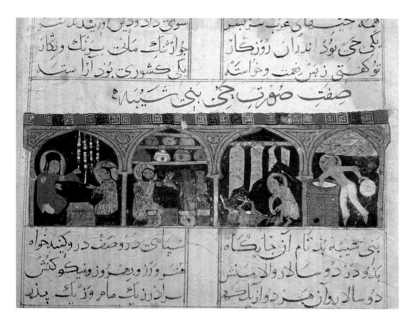

For example, "And whatever of character there is in a man, even though he thinks it concealed from people, it is known. . . . The tongue of a man is one half, and the other half is his mind, and there is nothing besides these two, except the shape of the blood and the flesh" (as posted on Fordham University's Medieval Islamic Sourcebook Web site).

One early form of Arabic poetry was the *qasida*. The *qasida* had three parts: the prologue, the journey, and the eulogy or invective. These odes told of desert journeys that took the narrator away from the people he loved, and his sense of sorrow at the separation. The *qasida* continued to be popular even after conquest began. Some of these poems were written by Arabs who yearned for their old lives in the desert.

In the early eighth century, Muslims learned the art of papermaking from Chinese captives. As paper became more readily available throughout the empire, the written word flourished. Before long, libraries to house these new works were being built in all the major cities.

Many of the caliphs supported poets. A common Islamic expression, "cutting off the tongue" of a poet, meant supporting the poet with money to prevent him from writing nasty poems about a person.

Two of the most important poets of the empire were Abu Nuwas (ca. 750–810) and Mutanabbi (915–965). Abu Nuwas wrote about love and wine, and was famous for his elegant use of language and his love of imagery. He was also famous for his drinking songs.

Mutanabbi was famous for his *qasida*, as well as poems praising those who supported him in flowery and highly descriptive language. His sarcastic political poems, however, often landed him in trouble. This is from a poem written to Syrian prince Sayf al-Dawla (as quoted on the Web site The Arab Washingtonian):

Poetry was an important part of Arabian culture even before the rise of Islam. This manuscript from about 1250 illustrates a scene from a poem. From the left, there are jewelers, an herbalist, butchers, and bakers.

Glory and honor were healed when you were healed, and your
   pain passed on to your enemies.
Light, that had left the sun, as if it was sick in its body, came
   back to it.
By race, the Arabs are supreme in the world, but a foreigner
   will take part with the Arabs of good heart.

Even some of the caliphs wrote a little poetry. Caliph Yazid composed a poem to his father that described how angry his father would become when Yazid was drinking. This is an excerpt:

'Twas sweet the flowing cup to seize,
'Tis sweet thy rage to see;
And first I drink myself to please;
And next—to anger thee.

PROSE

Contact with other cultures influenced Islamic literature, but style continued to be more important than form. For Islamic writers, the beauty of word and thought was most important. The earliest prose pieces in the Islamic Empire were translations of Persian works about the life and manners of courtiers. Later, the Muslims developed their own prose forms. As time passed, prose eventually became the most important way of recording the history and stories of the Islamic Empire.

One important form of Islamic literature is the *sira*, which is a biography of Muhammad. The first *sira* was written by Ibn Ishaq (ca. 704–773), and it remains one of the few full biographies of Muhammad.

People throughout the empire also enjoyed a type of literature called *adab*, which was meant for entertainment. *Adab* combined fun tales with an educational lesson or moral.

One of the first *adab* was *Kalila and Dimna* (750), a translation of some Indian fables. The tales, which were translated by Ibn al-Muqaffaa during the reign of Caliph al-Mansur, used animals to teach lessons to rulers. Unfortunately, the author was not as well-received as the work. Al-Mansur ordered the writer killed after he supported an uncle who rebelled against the caliph.

Omar al-Khayyam

Omar al-Khayyam (ca. 1048–1125) was a Persian Muslim mathematician and astronomer. He helped create an accurate solar calendar and was the first person to solve cubic equations. He gained his greatest fame, however, as a poet. Throughout his life, he composed more than 1,000 quatrains—poems in which each verse is made up of four lines. These poems were collected in the *Rubaiyyat of Omar Khayyam*. In 1859, Umar's masterpiece was translated into English. The poems rapidly gained popularity throughout the West, and are among the best-known works of poetry around the world.

Another popular type of literature was the *maqama*, or "literary assembly." *Maqamat* were adventures, told by a fictional narrator, using rhyming prose. Writers used *maqamat* as a way to criticize conditions in the world around them and offer moral lessons. Like poetry, the form of the *maqama* was more important than its content. As a record of what life was like in the medieval Islamic Empire, this form of literature has had a lasting impact.

Thousand and One Nights

The best-known piece of literature to come out of the Islamic Empire, for Westerners, is the *Thousand and One Nights*. The work is a collection of tales written by different authors over hundreds of years. The *Thousand and One Nights* gives a glimpse into what life was like in the Islamic Empire from the ninth through the 16th centuries.

The stories in the book include fairy tales from India and Persia, love stories from Egypt, and legends from Arabia. The tales from other countries and cultures were adapted by the authors to reflect Muslim traditions and customs. Familiar characters from the book include Ali Baba, Sinbad, and Aladdin. Although the work was widely read in the West after its translation into English in the 1840s, the *Thousand and One Nights* was not considered a great literary work by Muslims.

One of the most famous stories in the *Thousand and One Nights* is the story of Sinbad the sailor and his seven sea voyages. The story comes from ancient Persian folktales that were passed on orally for generations. The tale of Sinbad offers a glimpse into Islamic trade during the eighth and ninth centuries. In the book *The Arabs: A Short History*, Philip Hitti writes that some of Sinbad's adventures were based on actual reports of trading voyages made by Islamic merchants.

During his travels to India and other parts of the world, Sinbad experiences many wild and fantastic adventures. He is shipwrecked by a huge whale, attacked by a gigantic bird, and nearly squeezed to death by an enormous snake. He even dines with cannibals and lives to tell the tale. Sinbad eventually returns to Baghdad and becomes a wealthy merchant.

Today, the tale of Sinbad remains popular among people of all ages. The story has been turned into cartoons, movies, and books. The most recent version of the centuries-old tale was the animated Walt Disney Studios film *Sinbad*, released in 2003. Brad Pitt supplied Sinbad's voice.

ISLAMIC ART

The art of the Islamic Empire was unique, beautiful, and functional. Much of early Islamic art was created to beautify religious or everyday items. As in so many things, the Arabs were influenced by the other cultures they came into contact with during the conquest. In fact, there was no true Arab art form (other than poetry) before the expansion of the empire.

Religion was a key force in all aspects of life in the Islamic empire, and had a strong influence on art. During the early days of the empire, sculptures and images of people were prohibited in mosques and discouraged in general.

Although these restrictions eased in later years, Muhammad was often shown with his face covered and surrounded by a halo of flames. More commonly, images of people were found in such non-religious settings as bathhouses and harems. They were also more acceptable on pillows and carpets.

Two of the most common types of Islamic visual art were calligraphy and illuminated manuscripts. Calligraphy, which is the art of elegant, ornamental writing, was the most respected of all the Islamic art forms. Nothing was more worthy than to write the word of Allah. It was considered an act of worship in itself.

Over the centuries, copies of the Quran have given Islamic calligraphers an opportunity to produce some of their finest and most beautiful works of art. These copies were often decorated with floral and geometric patterns and panels between each chapter.

Those who wanted to excel at calligraphy studied for years under a master calligrapher. The master taught his students how to sit in a squatting position when writing, with the paper balanced on one knee. Students were taught one of the six classic styles of rounded Arabic writing.

One of the most important parts of being a calligrapher was learning how to properly cut a reed (a type of stiff plant stalk) to make a pen. Pens were so important that they were sometimes passed on from masters to favorite students. They also learned how to make ink out of indigo (blue dye), soot, and henna and how to put lines on paper.

Artists could make a profession of calligraphy. They made copies of the Quran, government documents, and books for libraries. They even wrote inscriptions on mosques, palaces, and tombs.

Much early Islamic art was created to decorate religious or everyday items. This bowl from the 10th or 11th century has a design of a bird.

Illumination is the art of creating brightly-colored miniature pictures. These miniatures were most commonly used to illustrate non-religious manuscripts. The first illuminations were used in Arabic translations of Greek works. They include pictures of plants, herbs, and animals from fables. Illumination was especially popular in Persia, Turkey, and India.

The Muslims also adopted the art forms of conquered peoples, particularly the use of decorative mosaics and carpet making. Other art forms that originally came from outside the empire include pottery, ivory and wood carving, glass making, and metal working with brass, bronze, gold, silver, and copper.

Beginning in the ninth century, ceramics became quite popular. Inspired by the fine Chinese porcelain that passed along Islamic trade routes, artists began creating finely-decorated plates, vases, and jugs. A luster (shiny) finish was very popular for these ceramic pieces. This was created by coating the pottery with metal oxides. After being heated, they took on a metallic shimmer. This process, called lustring, was eventually passed on to the West through Spain.

MUSIC IN THE EMPIRE

Most forms of Islamic music developed during the eighth through 10th centuries. As the empire grew, Arab music was influenced by other cultures around the empire. Syria, Egypt, Persia, and later Spain were especially influential.

Although the style of Arab music remained the same in many ways, it also borrowed aspects of the music from other areas. For this reason, classical Muslim music from Turkey is recognizably different from classical music from Morocco, Egypt, and other areas.

Muslim musicians were also heavily influenced by the ancient Greeks. As Greek works were translated into Arabic, music became respected as a science, similar to mathematics and astronomy. Arab scholars studied music, wrote books about it, and even created new theories about the technical aspects of music.

Despite the protests of conservative Muslims, who believed music was discouraged by Muhammad, music flourished in the royal courts of both the Umayyads and the Abbasids. Many musicians, like poets, were supported by the caliph and his court. Gifted musicians could earn fame and fortune throughout the empire.

The distinctive musical sound that is associated with Arabia is the result of the musical instruments that were first used throughout the Islamic Empire. The main instrument for music-making in the empire was the oud. Known as "the king of musical instruments" and the "prince of enchantment," the oud may have originated in Egypt or in the Sassanian Empire.

The oud was a pear-shaped instrument with a rounded back and a flat front. Early ouds, made of lightweight wood, had four strings made of silk or animal gut. The oud was held like a guitar and played with one or two picks that were attached to the forefinger. These picks were often made of trimmed eagle's feathers.

The oud was the only instrument to accompany the *sawt*, a type of song that was eventually spread into Western Europe by crusaders returning from the Empire. In the *sawt*, the audience chanted parts of a song in response to the singer. This style influenced troubadours, who were poet-musicians in Spain and France. The oud, which produced a deep sound, may even have been played on the battlefield.

One of the most famous musicians of the Islamic Empire was Ziryab (759–857), a freed slave from Baghdad who moved to Cordoba. In Spain, Ziryab became a well-known singer, teacher, and oud player. He combined Greek, Persian, and Arab influences in his compositions to create a style of music that was unique to Spain.

Ziryab was well-rewarded for his skills: The emir Abd al-Rahman II (788–852) gave him his own furnished mansion, gifts, and a monthly salary.

Another stringed instrument used in Arabic music-making was the *qanun*, a zither-like instrument descended from the Egyptian harp. Developed in the 10th century, the *qanun* was a flat wooden board with 25 to 27 sets of strings made from animal gut or silk. This versatile

"Oriental Dance"

For some American women, belly dancing has become a way to have fun and keep fit. Belly dancing, also known as *raks sharki,* or "oriental dance," has its roots in Arabia. There is some mystery, however, surrounding when and why *raks sharki* was first performed—particularly given the Islamic custom of modest dress for women. Some stories say the dance dates back to pre-Islamic days, when it was performed at weddings and other celebrations. Others believe the dance may have developed as a way for pregnant women to prepare their abdominal muscles for labor and birth. In some Islamic countries today, *raks sharki* is banned or discouraged.

CONNECTIONS

The Oud and the Guitar

The Arab musical instrument, the oud, led to the development of the lute in Spain. In fact, the word *lute* comes from the Arabic phrase *al oud*. The lute is a musical instrument with a pear-shaped body and six pairs of strings.

The lute and other stringed instruments helped create a new class of performing artists in Europe: minstrels and troubadours. These skilled musicians moved from city to city strumming on ouds and other instruments, singing ballads, folk songs, and Christmas carols. Troubadours became very popular and well-respected in royal courts throughout Europe in the 12th and 13th centuries.

The guitar, which is a member of the lute family, may also have originated in Spain. The word *guitar*, which comes from the Arabic word *qitara*, originally was used to describe a flat-backed, four-stringed instrument. The guitar was easier to play than the lute, and by the late 1500s, it had passed its cousin in popularity in Spain and other parts of Europe. As the years went on, a fifth and then a sixth string were added to the guitar.

The guitar and Arabic music influenced the development of flamenco music in the Andalusia region of Spain. Flamenco combines guitar music with singing, dancing, and rhythmic clapping to create a unique and dramatic performance style. Historians believe that Flamenco combines Arabic, Roma (Gypsy), and Spanish musical styles from the medieval period. Today, flamenco is still a popular art form in Spain.

instrument was played by plucking the strings with the fingers or with pieces of horn.

Percussion instruments included the *darbukka*, or *tabla*, a small hand-held drum made by stretching goat, calf, or fish skin over a large clay container. The *mihbaj* was a multi-functional Bedouin instrument that doubled as a coffee grinder. *The mihbaj* was about a foot tall, with a two-feet tall pestle (a rounded stick) used both for grinding coffee and making percussion sounds.

The *nay* was a simple reed pipe, similar to a flute, adapted from the Sumerians. The *nay* most often had six holes in the front, with one hole underneath for the thumb. It was one of the few wind instruments used in the Islamic Empire. During a performance, musicians might use as many as seven *nays* of different sizes to produce a variety of sounds.

ARCHITECTURE

One of the most lasting legacies of the Islamic Empire is the unique and distinctive architecture that still survives in many regions today. The most important architectural achievement throughout the history of the empire was the mosque. For Muslims in the Islamic Empire, the mosque served as a place to worship Allah, and much more. It was also the heart of the community. The mosque was a court of justice, a place for study, and even a shelter and place of sanctuary for weary travelers.

The oud is the ancestor to the lute and the guitar, and is still a popular instrument in Middle Eastern music.

The first mosque was the home of Muhammad in Medina. His home included a large, open courtyard and a covered area to shelter worshippers. The muezzin, or caller, climbed to the roof of Muhammad's home to call the faithful to worship. Later mosques were based on this first place of worship.

During the earliest days of the empire, some of the first mosques were former Christian churches. During the Umayyad dynasty, the construction of new mosques began.

These first mosques were designed by architects and built by craftsmen from around the empire: Arabs, Persians, Syrians, and Egyptians all contributed to the design and construction of early mosques. The designers incorporated some of the styles from their home region into the mosque's structure and design. In areas that were once part of the Byzantine Empire, for example, Turkish architects used domes and half domes when designing their mosques. In Persia, the walls were covered with colored ceramic tiles decorated with Persian patterns.

Throughout the empire, however, all mosques shared a number of basic characteristics. Most were rectangular, with an open courtyard and a covered prayer hall. During the Umayyad dynasty, a minaret, or tower, became standard for new mosques. Minarets may have been inspired by the lighthouse of Alexandria in Egypt, which was one of the

Mosque Facts

◆ The largest mosque built during the Islamic Empire was the Great Mosque at Samarra. It was begun by the Abbasid caliph al-Mutasim. The mosque covered 45,500 square yards. Inside, it was paved with marble and supported by marble columns, with enamel tiles covering the walls. The minaret (tower), which is the only feature of the mosque that survives today, was 175 feet tall.

◆ The Dome of the Rock is one of the oldest Islamic structures in the world. It was built in 691, less than six decades after the death of Muhammad. It remains one of the most breathtaking and beautiful sites in Jerusalem.

◆ One of the largest mosques in the world today is the Hassan II Mosque in Casablanca, Morocco. There is room for about 25,000 worshippers inside the mosque, while 80,000 more can gather outside. Its minaret, the tallest in the world, stretches more than 680 feet into the sky. Construction on the mosque began in 1986 and it was finished in 1993.

Seven Wonders of the Ancient World. The muezzin made his call to prayer from the minaret.

Another important mosque feature, the mihrab, was added around the beginning of the eighth century. The mihrab, or prayer niche, enables every Muslim throughout the empire to locate the *qibla*, the direction of Mecca. This is where Muslims face when they pray. The mihrab is usually beautifully decorated, with much attention paid to its design.

Other mosque characteristics included a fountain for cleansing. In many cases, the mosque's fountain also served as the main well for the town.

The imam, or religious leader, stood on the *minbar*, a sort of pulpit, to lead the people in prayer. The side of the mosque closest to Mecca was the site of the sanctuary, which was the meeting place for the community. There is no law that requires Muslims to worship in a mosque. However, the mosque enables worshippers to unite as a community of people.

In mosques throughout the Islamic Empire (and in most mosques today), there are separate sections where women may worship apart from the men. In the early days of the empire, most women prayed at home. Later, they stood at the back of the mosque and left before the men. Finally, special sections were set aside for them to pray. However, while it is common for Muslim women to pray at the mosque in Western countries, most Muslim women around the world still pray at home.

Some of the most notable examples of early Umayyad mosques that are still around today are the Dome of the Rock and the Aqsa Mosque in Jerusalem, and the Great Mosque in Damascus. These large, beautiful structures helped the Umayyads make their claim that they were the successors of Muhammad and the leaders of the *umma*. The mosques were all built to outshine Christian churches that stood nearby.

The caliph al-Walid, who commissioned the Great Mosque in Damascus, did not want Muslims to be distracted by churches. Al-Walid's mosque was therefore built over the site of a Christian church. The church's towers were converted into minarets.

These early mosques were made of stone, and included such features as mosaic tiles, and decorative patterns. As more mosques were constructed throughout the empire, they became even more beautiful and elaborate.

Although Islam forbids statues or portraits of people in mosques, other designs were used to decorate the mosques. These included geometric patterns, floral and plant patterns (a Byzantine influence), and animals such as birds, antelopes, lions, dogs, and mythological creatures from Persian tradition, such as griffins (the body of a lion and the head and wings of an eagle) and dragons.

One of the most beautiful mosques in the Islamic Empire was the Great Mosque of Cordoba, built in 785 by emir Abd al-Rahman I, the Umayyad prince who had escaped the Abbasid slaughter of his family. Abd al-Rahman called his mosque the Kaaba of the West. Muslims and Christians alike considered it one of the wonders of the medieval world.

The mosque was built on the site where a Christian church and, before that, a Roman temple had stood. It was modeled on Umayyad mosques in Syria and Palestine. Marble taken from nearby Roman ruins supplied the material for 500 columns within the mosque. The columns gave visitors the sensation of being in a forest of stone. Another striking feature of the mosque was its two-level, horseshoe-shaped, red and white archways. Other unique decorative elements included the mosaic on the mihrab and a main dome decorated with gold mosaic cubes.

The Great Mosque of Cordoba was expanded over about two centuries. At one point, it was the third largest mosque in the Islamic Empire. After the Christian Spanish kings took control of Cordoba in 1236, a cathedral was built in the heart of the mosque. Today, the mosque's minaret is part of the cathedral's bell tower.

Second only to mosques were the royal palaces. The first caliphs to build royal palaces were the Umayyads. They erected big, strong complexes on the edges of the desert near Syria and Jordan. Early palaces included central courtyards, walls, towers, and a gate. Arcades (covered walkways) ran around the open courtyard. Inside were a throne room, a reception room, and living areas for the caliph and his family and courtiers. Early royal complexes often included a large bathhouse decorated with mosaic-tiled floors.

When the Abbasids took power, they had to outdo their predecessors. In Baghdad and other cities throughout the empire, the caliphs built huge palaces made of brick. These palaces became even larger and more heavily decorated as the Abbasids lost true political power.

Without an empire to run, the Abbasid caliphs turned their attention to spending the wealth of the kingdom on extravagant palaces and other buildings. In Samarra, for example, the Jawsaq Palace, begun in 836, covered more than 430 acres. It included reception rooms, living quarters, harem quarters for the women, pools, gardens, and fountains in the courtyard.

One of the most luxurious royal residences ever built in the empire was the Abbasid palace in Baghdad. The design of the palace was strongly influenced by Persian culture. Visitors approached the wonderful marble building through a golden gate.

The palace was surrounded by gardens with fountains, sculpture, blooming trees, and a variety of plants. There was also a zoo on the grounds that was home to the many wild, exotic animals collected by the Abbasids. The palace's crowning achievement was the 120-foot-tall green dome, topped by a statue of a horseman holding a lance.

Inside, goods from all over the empire decorated each room. Tapestries (thick fabric woven with pictures) and brocades (silk woven with raised patterns) stitched with gold thread hung from the walls. Mosaic tiles, colored glass, carved wood, and stucco (plaster) carvings could be seen everywhere.

For a special occasion, one Abbasid caliph created the Hall of the Tree to hold a huge artificial tree of gold and silver. On the branches, mechanical silver and gold birds sang tunes for astounded guests.

STOREHOUSE OF KNOWLEDGE

During the Abbasid dynasty, the Islamic Empire became known as the light of the world. Here, knowledge and learning were nurtured and encouraged. Arabic translations of Greek works, along with Islamic advances in learning, laid the foundations for modern science, medicine, and other fields of learning.

CONNECTIONS

Scientific Words with Arabic Origins

alchemy: from *al-kimiya*, which means the sciences of alchemy and chemistry; in English it means the "science" of trying to turn ordinary metals into gold

alcohol: from *al-kuhl*, which means ground cosmetic powder; it was later used to describe refined or distilled substances

algebra: from *al-jabr*, which means the joining together of disorganized parts

borax: from *buraq*, a white, powdery mineral used in cleaning and soldering

camphor: from *kafur*, a strong-smelling tree gum often used in medical ointments

elixir: from *al-iksir*, in medieval alchemy, a material that would change other metals to gold; in English it means a magical potion

nadir: from *nazir*, the lowest point

pancreas: from *bancras*

zenith: from *samt*, the highest point

zero: from *sifr*, which was translated into Latin as *zephyrum* and then into Italian as *zero*

Many Greek works were translated during the reign of Caliph Al-Mamun (r. 813–833). Some of these Greek works were taken when Muslims conquered Byzantine and Sassanian areas. In other cases, the caliphs sent out groups of scholars to find Greek writings in other cities, including Constantinople.

To help scholars translate and study these works, al-Mamun founded the House of Wisdom in Baghdad. The House of Wisdom included a library, a translation bureau, and a school. There was also an observatory from which scholars and scientists could study the stars and planets—and even discover new ones.

At its height, the House of Wisdom had as many as 90 scholars working on translations. These translations eventually made their way to Muslim Spain and Sicily, and from there, to the Western world, where they were translated into Latin. This preserved the vast wealth of knowledge of the ancient masters.

PHILOSOPHY AND HISTORY

Many important Islamic philosophers emerged in the ninth century. Islamic philosophy, like other areas of knowledge, was profoundly influenced by the Greek masters. Islamic philosophers most frequently focused on themes that touched on religion, especially the relationship of logic and reasoning to the Quran and sunna.

One of the most famous philosophers of the empire was Abu al-Walid Muhammad ibn Rushd (1126–1198), known in the West as Averroës. Ibn Rushd was born in Cordoba, Spain, while it was under Muslim control. As a young man, he studied the works of the ancient Greeks, including Aristotle and Plato. He later served as the caliph's doctor and a judge.

One of Ibn Rushd's most famous works of philosophy was *On the Harmony of Religions and Philosophy*, written in 1190. The book includes chapters on "The Creation of the Universe," "Divine Justice and Injustice," and "The Day of Judgment." However, his thoughts on the soul and other religious matters covered in the book got him into trouble with Muslim authorities. His views did not follow the strict interpretations of Islam. He was declared a heretic (someone whose opinions do not follow accepted ideas) and was banished from Cordoba in 1195.

IN THEIR OWN WORDS

Honoring the Ancient Masters

Abu al-Walid Muhammad ibn Rushd (1126–1198), known in the West as Averroës, was a famous philosopher. As a young man, he studied the works of the ancient Greeks. In this excerpt from his most famous book, *On the Harmony of Religions and Philosophy*, he explains why studying the ancient Greek philosophers is important. If what they say is true, we can learn from it. If what they say is false, then we know what not to believe. Deciding what is true and what is not gives us the tools we need to understand the universe.

All that is wanted in an enquiry into philosophical reasoning has already been perfectly examined by the Ancients. All that is required of us is that we should go back to their books and see what they have said in this connection. If all that they say be true, we should accept it and if there be something wrong, we should be warned by it. Thus, when we have finished this kind of research we shall have acquired instruments by which we can observe the universe, and consider its general character. For so long as one does not know its general character one cannot know the created, and so long as he does not know the created, he cannot know its nature.

(Source: Averroës. "Kitab fasl al-maqal (On the harmony of religions and philosophy)." Medieval Sourcebook. Available online. URL: http://www.fordham.edu/halsall/source/1190averroes.html#Introduction. Accessed March 12, 2008.)

Ibn Rushd's works were eventually translated into Latin, the language of European scholars at the time. They provided the foundation for a famous work of theology (the study of the nature of God and religion) begun in 1265 by Catholic scholar Thomas Aquinas. Aquinas's work, *Summa Theologica*, is considered one of the greatest philosophical book to come out of Europe during the Middle Ages.

The most famous Islamic historian was al-Biruni (973–1048). In addition to writing one of the first Arab histories, Biruni was also a noted geographer and scientist. His *Chronology*, written in 1030, offered an account of the histories of ancient empires of the world. It included information on their festivals, calendars, and rituals. His most famous work was *Kitab al-Hind*, a book that described the history and geography of India.

IN THEIR OWN WORDS

A History of the World

Al-Biruni (973–1048) was one of the most famous Muslim historians. His book *Chronology* started all the way at the beginning of time, with the creation of humans. In this excerpt, he complains that not much is known for certain about this event. The different religions offer different stories, and it happened so long ago that no one can remember it clearly.

The first and most famous of the beginnings of antiquity is the fact of the creation of mankind. But among those who have a book of divine revelation, such as the Jews, Christians, Magians, and their various sects, there exists such a difference of opinion as to the nature of this fact, and as to the question how to date from it, the like of which is not allowable for eras. Everything, the knowledge of which is connected with creation and with the history of bygone generations, is mixed up with falsifications and myths, because it belongs to a far remote age; because a long interval separates us therefrom, and because the student is incapable of keeping it in memory, and of fixing it (so as to preserve it from confusion).

(Source: Horne, Charles F. *The Sacred Books and Early Literature of the East.* New York: Parke, Austin & Lipscomb, 1917.)

ADVANCES IN MEDICINE

Some of the most important contributions of the Islamic Empire came in the field of medicine. By applying and adding to Greek medical theory, the doctors of the empire were the most advanced of their time. European crusaders who came into contact with Islamic medicine brought home some of the treatments they learned about. These helped advance European medical practices of the day.

Most early Islamic doctors were Persian. The Persians had adopted the Greek medical ideas of Galen and Hippocrates, two Greek scientists, before the Muslim conquest.

One of the most talented and learned Persian physicians was al-Razi (ca. 865–925). Razi wrote more than 100 medical books. He was the first person to document the symptoms of smallpox, thus explaining how it was different from other similar diseases. This made diagnosis and treatment of the disease more effective. Al-Razi also wrote about immobilizing broken bones using a plaster substance, so they could heal more effectively.

Al-Razi was especially interested in the relationship between hygiene and sickness. Many centuries before germs and bacteria were identified, this Islamic doctor believed that sick people should be kept in a clean environment. His most famous work was a huge, private notebook of medical essays that included Greek, Persian, Syrian, Hindu, and Arabic information. The book was called *Kitab al-Hawi fi al-tibb* (comprehensive book on medicine), and it influenced medical practices throughout Europe.

People throughout the empire took the practice of medicine quite seriously. Not just anyone could become a doctor. Men had to have special training and pass tests on anatomy and the writings of Galen. Specialists had to have even more knowledge of the field in which they were practicing. Beginning in 931, some caliphs required doctors to be licensed.

Islamic doctors used a number of methods to treat sick patients, including acupuncture, drugs, and ointments. Some treatments seem remarkably similar to ones used today. For example, a physician might recommend that a patient with a stomach problem follow a special diet. Someone with a serious wound might be prescribed a healing poultice (a warm mash of herbs) or ointment.

However, some treatments were quite unusual by today's standards. In addition to bloodletting (drawing out blood from the veins), doctors might try cupping—placing hot glasses on the skin's surface to draw the blood upward. Cupping, which was also practiced in Asia, was thought to be good for curing headaches and purifying the blood.

Doctors made medicines out of a wide variety of materials. They used balsam, ginger, and various fruits, plants, and herbs to create healing potions. Some drugs were made with animal and metal products. Although most doctors mixed up their own medicines and ointments, there were also pharmacies, where mixing and storing drugs was overseen by an inspector.

Islamic doctors performed various types of surgeries. These were usually based on ancient Greek methods. Surgeons used drainage tubes, anesthetics (including opium), and cauterization (burning flesh to stop bleeding)—techniques that are still used today.

They amputated diseased arms and legs and operated on cataracts of the eyes. In fact, ophthalmology, the medical study of the eye, was one area in which Islamic physicians excelled. The first book on ophthalmology and the eye's structure and functions was written by Hunayn ibn Ishaq, a Persian who studied medicine in Baghdad during the middle of the ninth century.

Physician Abu Ali al-Hasan ibn al-Haytham (965–ca. 1040), known as Alhazen in the West, is remembered today as the father of optics (the study of light). He discovered that vision is the result of rays of light reflecting off objects and passing into the eye.

A doctor takes blood from a patient as a large crowd watches in this 13th-century Iraqi manuscript. Important advances in medicine were made during the Islamic Empire.

The first Islamic hospital was built in Baghdad in the early ninth century. Before long, there were more than 30 hospitals throughout the empire. In remote areas, traveling clinics set up tents and sick villagers were treated and medicated, if necessary.

At hospitals, any sick person, regardless of their culture or religion, would be treated. In the larger hospitals, patients were separated into wards depending upon their illness. There was also a special ward for the mentally ill. Islamic hospitals also had something similar to the modern-day emergency room. Here, minor illnesses that did not require hospitalization were treated.

The most famous physician of the Islamic Empire was Abu Ali al-Husayn ibn Sina (980–1037), known in the West as Avicenna. Ibn Sina was born near Bukhara (in what is today Uzbekistan). He began

CONNECTIONS

Monumental Medical Advances

Islamic contributions to medicine were monumental. Many of the practices that Muslim doctors described, improved, or pioneered are still used today in one form or another. Advances in medicine during the empire included:

The pharmacy: In *A History of the Arab Peoples*, Albert Hourani writes, "It has been said that the pharmacy as an institution is an Islamic invention." Because of the vast Islamic trading network, Muslim doctors had access to many new drugs. Muslim scholars wrote books about the properties and effects of a wide variety of drugs. They were also the first to create a systematic method of determining dosages for medicines. Pharmacol-ogy was considered an important profession. Beginning in the early 800s, pharmacists, like doctors, had to pass examinations and become licensed.

Surgical milestones: At a time when European clergymen were encouraging doctors to stop performing any type of surgery, Muslim doctors were moving ahead in successful efforts to cure their patients surgically. They performed operations to remove bladder stones, cataracts and other eye diseases, and varicose veins. They also created many new surgical instruments and pioneered the use of anesthesia, especially opium, to make a patient unconscious before surgery. The anesthesia was administered by

practicing medicine when he was just 18 years old. He later served as the personal doctor to the sultan of Bukhara. Over the years, Ibn Sina also became interested in philosophy, physics, mathematics, astronomy, and even music theory.

Milestones in Ibn Sina's career include his descriptions of skin diseases and psychological illnesses. He was the first person to realize that tuberculosis can be spread from person to person, and that some diseases are spread by water and soil. For cancer, his treatment is still followed today: Treat the illness during its earliest stages and remove all the diseased tissue.

Ibn Sina's best-known work was *Al-Qanafi'l Tibb* (the canon of medicine). This encyclopedia of medical knowledge was studied throughout the Islamic Empire and in European universities from the 12th through the 17th centuries.

holding a drug-soaked sponge underneath the patient's nose.

Understanding disease: The Muslims were among the first to understand that many diseases are contagious. In the 14th century, Ibn al-Khatib described how disease is spread (quoted in Bernard Lewis's *A Middle East Mosaic*): "The existence of contagion is established by experience, study, and the evidence of the senses, by trustworthy reports on transmission by garments, vessels, ear-rings; by the spread of it by persons from one house, by infection of a healthy sea-port by an arrival from an infected land." Muslim doctors were the first to describe the differences between smallpox and measles, and to identify scabies and anthrax.

Hygiene and health: Some of the most important contributions to medical knowledge by Islamic physicians came in the field of hygiene and its relationship to health. They were the first to describe the germ-killing effects of alcohol and to use it in hospitals. The idea of a healthy environment was also pioneered by the Muslims. To determine the healthiest place for a new hospital in Baghdad, the famous physician al-Razi hung slabs of meat in various parts of the city. The area where the meat rotted most slowly was chosen as the hospital's new site.

Record keeping: Islamic hospitals were probably among the first to keep medical records on all patients. The records included information on the patient's condition and treatment.

ASTRONOMY AND THE ISLAMIC CALENDAR

Astronomy, the study of the stars and the planets, was an important field of study in the Islamic Empire. Astronomy was a useful science because it helped people find their way on land or at sea. Astronomy was also approved by the Quran (Sura 6, verse 97), which states, "[Allah] has appointed for you the stars, that by them you might be guided in the shadows of land and sea" (quoted on the Web site World Scripture).

Arabs had always been interested in the sky. Early Arabs named certain planets and stars, using these heavenly bodies to guide them safely across the desert. After the conquest began, Islamic scholars used information learned from the ancient peoples of Persia, Greece, and India to improve and advance the field of astronomy.

CONNECTIONS

Contributions to Astronomy

Islamic scientists excelled in astronomy. Al-Battani (ca. 858–929) more precisely calculated the length of a solar year than anyone had ever done before. He calculated it was 365 days, 5 hours, 46 minutes, 24 seconds. The most recent modern measurement is 365 days, 5 hours, 48 minutes, and 45.5 seconds. The Polish astronomer Copernicus (1473–1543), who proposed the theory that all planets in the solar system rotate around the Sun, mentioned in one of his books that he learned a great deal from the work of al-Battani.

Islamic scientists were the first to use the observatory (a special building for watching the skies) as a scientific institution. From observatories in Baghdad, Cairo, and other places in the empire, Abul Wafa (940–998) and other astronomers watched and described the movements of the Sun, planets, and stars. In the 16th century, Danish scientist Tycho Brahe (1546–1601) watched the movements of the Moon and made the same discoveries Islamic astronomers had made centuries earlier. From an observatory in Egypt, al-Battani catalogued close to 500 stars.

As the empire was being torn apart in the early 1250s, Islamic scholars continued to make advances in the field of astronomy. In 1274, Muslim astronomer Nasir al-Din al-Tusi (1201–1274) convinced the Mongol invaders to allow him to build a huge observatory in what is today northwest Iran. The observatory at Maraghah was a center for astronomical research for many years and provided a model for future observatories.

One way in which astronomy affected the Islamic Empire was through the Islamic calendar. This calendar is based on the cycles of the Moon. This is different from the Gregorian calendar used by most Western countries today, which is based on the movements of the Sun.

Like the Gregorian calendar, the Islamic calendar has 12 months. These months alternate between 29 and 30 days each. There are also leap years. Because it is a lunar calendar, though, the Islamic calendar falls about 11 days behind the solar calendar each year. As a result, the Islamic calendar does not follow the seasons.

The Islamic calendar was created in 638 by the order of Caliph Umar. Umar wanted the calendar to begin with the year 1 being the Hijra, Muhammad's migration to Medina and the birth of Islam. Therefore, in the Islamic calendar every date after July 16, 622, is marked A.H., which means after the Hijra.

GEOGRAPHY

The Islamic Empire was much more advanced in its knowledge of geography than were other regions of the world at that time. The need to advance in this field of learning was driven by the size of the empire. Travelers from one area to another needed accurate maps and guidebooks to help them get where they needed to go. As a result, guidebooks with the names of roads, towns, and distances from one place to another became quite common. Guidebooks were written about other lands as well, including China, India, and Russia.

Muslim mapmakers worked together with astronomers to produce a view of the sky and the Earth that was more accurate and comprehensive than ever before. As a result, maps from the Islamic Empire were highly valued by ship's captains throughout the world.

Muslim explorers also had a number of other advantages. For example, Islamic sailors used lateen sails—triangular sails that made their ships faster than ships using square sails.

The astrolabe was an ancient Greek invention used to pinpoint the position of stars. It was widely used by Muslim scholars. Called "the mathematical jewel," the astrolabe consisted of a flat metal disk with degrees marked around the outer edge. A pivot (a central pin) and pointer were attached at the instrument's center. By pointing the astrolabe at the stars, scientists were able to determine their positions and the movement of the planets.

Islamic scientists also calculated the circumference (the width around the center) and diameter (the length from a point in the middle of the globe to the outside edge) of the Earth more accurately than ever before. They came within 4 percent of the Earth's actual circumference.

A Different Calendar

The Islamic calendar is still used in most Muslim countries today as a religious calendar, to mark festivals and holidays. New days begin at sunset, and new months begin with the first visible crescent of the new moon. The Islamic months are:

1. Muharram
2. Safar
3. Rabi al-Awwal
4. Rabi al-Thani
5. Jumada al-Uda
6. Jumada al-Thaniyya
7. Rajab
8. Shaban
9. Ramadan
10. Shawwal
11. Dhu al-Qada
12. Dhu al-Hijja

MATHEMATICS, CHEMISTRY, AND PHYSICS

Mathematics was a field of knowledge that had many applications in the ancient Islamic world. It assisted scholars studying astronomy, and had the more practical uses of aiding in trade, commerce, and surveying (marking out the borders of land).

Some of the most basic mathematical concepts, including Arabic numerals, the idea of zero, and the decimal system, were spread to the West through the Islamic Empire. These concepts enabled people to work with large numbers without having to use words or letters. However, they

CONNECTIONS

Making Sense of Math

Many of the mathematical theories developed during the height of the Islamic Empire advanced the disciplines of arithmetic, geometry, algebra, and other branches of mathematics. Perhaps most important, Muslim scholars made mathematics useful and practical.

The Muslims owed much of their early knowledge of mathematics to texts written by ancient Greeks and Hindus. Islamic scholars then expanded upon this Greek and Hindu information, developing and advancing concepts and theories. Centuries later, texts written in the Islamic Empire would inspire and teach European scholars.

One of the most significant Islamic contributions to math was popularizing a new system of numerals borrowed from the Hindus. These numerals, which are now known as Arabic numerals, are the same symbols that are used today for numbers. Before this time, numbers were represented with letters of the alphabet or with Roman numerals, which were difficult to work with.

The new numeral system enabled merchants and others to more quickly and efficiently solve math problems without the use of an abacus (a counting device using beads strung on wires) or a process known as "finger reckoning." (Finger reckoning, or counting on the fingers, was widely used by merchants before the introduction of Arabic numerals.) By using the new numbers, problems could now be solved with pen and paper.

A second important Muslim contribution to mathematics also originated with the Hindus. It was a system of arithmetic based on 10 and included zero. Before the use of zero, those solving math problems had to arrange their numbers in columns to make clear their different values. The use of the base-10 system and zero made arithmetic logical and practical, and was adopted by European mathematicians centuries later. The zero also enabled Muslim scholars to further develop the decimal system and fractions.

Muslims also advanced other Hindu concepts, taking square and cube roots to fourth, fifth, and even higher roots.

Another branch of mathematics that blossomed during the Islamic Empire was algebra. Algebra (which comes from the Arabic term *al-jabr*, or "the joining together of disorganized parts"), was more fully developed by Muslim mathematicians. They pioneered the use of linear, quadratic, and cubic equations. They also devised a step-by-step process to solve problems, called an algorithm. The concept of "x" as the unknown variable in algebraic equations came about from a Spanish translation of the Arabic word *shay*, or "thing." Geometry and trigonometry were also advanced by Muslim scholars.

were borrowed from other cultures. For example, Arabic numerals, used for numbers today, were taken from the Hindus.

Islamic scholars enjoyed puzzling over difficult mathematical concepts and equations. They even created puzzles for one another to solve. Some of these puzzles are still worked on by mathematicians today. The love of advanced mathematical concepts led to advancements in algebra, geometry, and trigonometry—all areas that had been originally developed by the ancient Greeks. The Muslim scholar al-Khwarizmi (ca. 780–850) wrote an algebra textbook that was used in Europe until the 16th century.

Islamic scholars also made major contributions to the field of chemistry, although it was by accident. Throughout the empire, men worked to turn ordinary metals such as iron into gold through a combination of magic and science. This study was known as alchemy, and it was the medieval predecessor of chemistry.

They were never successful. But through alchemy, scientists of the Islamic Empire made a number of advances that contributed greatly to the development of modern science, particularly chemistry and physics. These scientists translated and studied the works of ancient Greek, Persian, and Indian scholars, then developed and enhanced them. But scientists throughout the empire—Muslims, Christians, and Jews—also made many original contributions to the sciences.

Alchemists also gained a better understanding of metallic compounds and how they are formed. They also developed information on refining metals, dyeing cloth, distilling vinegar, and manufacturing glass.

One of the outstanding minds of the Islamic Empire was a man named Jabir ibn Hayyan, known to the West as Geber (ca. 721–815). Ibn Hayyan (and later, those writing under his name) improved a variety of methods used in chemistry experiments, including crystallization, distillation, and evaporation. He also prepared a number of new chemical substances. His books are among the oldest known works on chemistry, and Ibn Hayyan is sometimes called "the father of chemistry."

Another important Islamic scientist and philosopher was al-Kindi (ca. 801–873), who wrote more than 200 works on physics and other matters. Topics that interested al-Kindi included optics (the reflection of light), weights, meteorology, and tides. Nearly four centuries after his death, al-Kindi's book on optics, *De Somniorum Visione*, served as a resource for other prominent scientists.

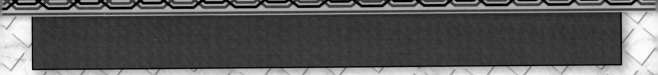

EPILOGUE

DESPITE THE FACT THAT THE MONGOL CONQUEST destroyed the Islamic Empire by about 1260, the power of Islam remained strong. Eventually the Mongol conquerors became Muslims themselves. Within 50 years, the Mongol rulers of Persia and Iraq had named Islam as their state religion. Although the empire itself was dead, Islam was still alive and was gaining converts throughout the Middle East, Africa, and Asia. In the coming centuries it continued to expand, spreading to all corners of the world.

One of the last great Islamic states was the Ottoman Empire, which eventually controlled Asia Minor and the Balkans. The Ottomans claimed the title of caliph in the 16th century. They redefined the term and the requirements of office to suit the fact that they were not members of the Quraysh.

The Ottoman Empire lasted until 1922. After that time, many nations that had once been part of the Islamic Empire fell under European control, becoming colonies of countries such as Great Britain and France. During the struggles to gain self-government, the idea of taking up arms in a jihad against the West gained strength among many Muslims.

The 20th century witnessed a revitalization of Islam. Following World War II, most of the colonies gained their independence from the European powers. These included all the Middle Eastern states, which were predominantly Muslim (except Israel and Lebanon).

Some states, such as Turkey and Tunisia, turned away from certain Islamic traditions. They preferred to have a state based on secular (nonreligious) politics and law. Other nations returned to the idea of Islam as both a religion and a guiding political force. In the middle of the 20th century,

OPPOSITE
Worshippers at a mosque in Jakarta, Indonesia. Muslims are found all over the world, and today, the majority of Muslims are not Arabs.

Iran: A Modern Theocracy

There are very few modern theocracies—governments run by religious leaders and according to religious law. One is the Islamic Republic of Iran. Since 1979, Iran's government has been headed by a Muslim religious and political leader called the *faqih*. The *faqih* is appointed by an assembly of experts and holds his job for life. He is the ultimate expert in interpreting Islamic law and how it applies to Iran's government. The *faqih* has the power to accept or reject any laws passed by the rest of the government. He also controls the country's armed forces and the judiciary system.

Iran also has an elected president and several appointed cabinet ministers. The president is the second most important person in Iran, after the *faqih*. According to Iran's constitution, the president must be a Shiite Muslim. He has the power to appoint ministers, sign laws, and reject any actions taken by the cabinet ministers.

All civil and criminal law in Iran is based on Shiite Islamic law. Chief justices, judges, and attorney generals must be religious men.

a number of states sprang up that included Islamic law in their legal codes. These include Pakistan (established in 1947; Islamic law came into effect in 1977), Indonesia (1949), Sudan (established in 1956; Islamic law came into effect in 1983), and Malaysia (1963).

The 20th century also marked the birth of two Muslim theocratic governments in Iran (1979) and Afghanistan (1996). In these two nations, the chief Islamic religious leader was also the recognized head of government. As in the time of the Islamic Empire, government and law were based on sharia. (The radical Islamic government of the Taliban in Afghanistan was ousted in 2001, although the country still identifies itself as an Islamic republic.)

With the break-up of the former Soviet Union in 1991, Central Asian states with large Muslim populations also emerged onto the world scene. Such nations include Uzbekistan, Turkmenistan, Tajikistan, and Azerbaijan.

Islam continues to be a strong political force around the globe and a unifying factor, drawing people from many nations together with the common bond of a shared religion. In 1969, the Organization of the Islamic Conference (OIC) was founded by 30 Islamic states to represent Muslim nations around the world. In 2009, 57 nations were part of the OIC. The group's stated mission (as quoted on the OIC Web site) is to "speak with one voice to safeguard the interest and ensure the progress and well-being of their peoples and other Muslims in the world over."

SHIITES AND SUNNIS

The split between Sunnis and Shiites dates back to divisions arising during the first century of Islam, when some Muslims felt that the proper successor to Muhammad was his cousin Ali, rather than his companion Abu Bakr. Since Sunnis and Shiites hold similar beliefs, the division between them over the centuries has been mostly political. For the majority of Islamic history, Sunni and Shiite communities have coexisted mostly peacefully, though each typically considers the other to be practicing Islam incorrectly.

Shiites have been the minority population in most parts of the Muslim world at most times in history. They have developed strategies for living under Sunni rule, despite the fact that they technically consider any Sunni government to be illegitimate. One of these strategies is the doctrine of *taqiyya*, which allows Shiites to deny that they follow Shiite

 CONNECTIONS

English Words, Arabic Roots

Every day, every time we speak, the lasting impact of the Islamic Empire can be heard in the hundreds of words that have Arabic roots. These words include the following:

ENGLISH	ARABIC	ENGLISH	ARABIC
admiral	*amir al* (commander of)	jar	*jarra* (earthen water vessel)
alcove	*al-qubba* (arch)	magazine	*makhazin* (storehouse)
almanac	*al-manakh*	massage	*massa* (to stroke)
apricot	*al-birquq*	mattress	*matrah* (place where something is thrown)
artichoke	*al-kharshuf*	safari	*safari* (journey)
candy	*qandi* (crystallized sugar)	sequin	*sikka* (place where coins are minted)
coffee	*qahwa*	sofa	*suffa* (carpet, divan)
cotton	*qutun*	syrup	*sharab*
ghoul	*ghul*	tabby	from *al-Attabiya*, a district in Baghdad where striped cloth was made
giraffe	*zirafa*		
guitar	*qitar*		

A young man in Baghdad rides his bicycle past a poster showing Islamic fundamentalist leaders. The division between moderate, progressive Muslims and conservative and fundamentalist groups has lead to conflict.

doctrine when they are challenged by Sunni authorities—although they continue to maintain Shiite beliefs in their hearts.

Most violence between Sunnis and Shiites over the centuries has arisen when Shiite communities have seemed strong enough to challenge Sunni rule. This has happened several times throughout history. One recent example is the Islamic Revolution of Iran in 1979, in which fundamentalist Shiites took power. This led to warfare between Iran and Iraq from 1980 to 1988. Iraq has a majority Shiite population, but the government was controlled by Sunnis. Iraqi leader Saddam Hussein feared that the Iranian revolution might inspire similar revolts among the Shiite community of Iraq.

The United States's invasion of Iraq in 2003 sparked violence between Sunnis and Shiites, as Sunnis grew concerned that their decades-long hold on power would be lost as a result of American influence. Shiite communities in Iraq also feel considerable resentment toward Sunnis, due to the oppression they have experienced under Sunni rule. This violence is likely to continue until one of the communities triumphs over the other or until an arrangement is made through which both communities feel their interests are protected.

Other inter-communal violence among Muslims throughout the world, particularly in Africa, often has to do with differing interpretations of the proper form of Islamic government. The rise of Islamist movements that seek to establish strict interpretations of Islamic law (sharia) as the law of the land has contributed to this violence. Sometimes this situation has been made worse by the involvement of outside powers, such as American military assistance for Afghan *mujahidin* (holy warriors) who fought against invaders from the Soviet Union throughout the 1980s. This American support directly (though accidentally) contributed to the rise of the extremist Taliban government when the Soviets pulled out of the country in 1989.

Likewise, financial assistance to Islamist movements throughout Africa by the government of Saudi Arabia has led to clashes between Muslim communities as well as violence between Muslims and Christians. In some cases, government oppression of Islamist movements has led to extensive violence. This was the case in Algeria and Egypt in the 1990s. The lack of political freedom in most Muslim countries directly contributes to this situation, since opposition groups often feel that they have no choice but to pursue power through violent means.

Jihad Today

Today, many Americans think of bloodshed and violence when they hear the word *jihad*. Jihad, however, means more than just holy war. It also means a constant struggle or striving on behalf of God. In the earliest days of Islam, it meant the struggle to live the way God commanded, to resist sin and wrongdoing, and to act justly. It also included sacrificing one's life—if necessary—in that struggle, as a *shahid*, or martyr.

Later, jihad came to mean the wars of conquest to spread the word of Muhammad. Jihad also requires Muslims to wage war when the *umma* (the Muslim community) is threatened by invasion, foreign rule, or forced conversion. Then they are defending their faith.

While some Muslims do interpret jihad in a broader, bloodier sense, most do not. Examples of extremist groups who have used the term jihad include the Jamaat al-Islamiyya in Palestine, the Muslim Brotherhood in Egypt, and al-Qaeda, an international terrorist group led by Osama bin Laden. These three groups, as well as several others, have caused death and destruction around the world. Most Muslims believe these extremist views misrepresent true Islamic teachings and values.

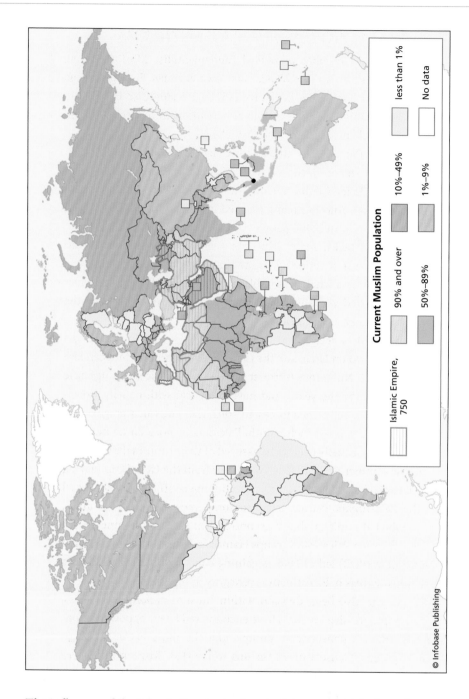

Current Muslim Population

Islamic Empire, 750

90% and over

50%–89%

10%–49%

1%–9%

less than 1%

No data

© Infobase Publishing

The influence of the Islamic Empire is clear in this map, which shows how many nations continue to embrace Islam after the empire crumbled.

THE CHALLENGE OF FUNDAMENTALISM

In recent years, a number of radical fundamentalist Muslim groups have taken up terrorism to advance their own agendas. Such groups as al-Qaeda, led by Osama bin Laden (b. 1957), have identified the United States, Saudi Arabia, and other nations as corrupting influences on Islam, and have made them targets of terrible violence.

One of the most deadly attacks took place on September 11, 2001. Terrorists from the al-Qaeda network hijacked planes and flew them into the World Trade Center in New York and the Pentagon building in Washington, D.C. Another plane crashed in Pennsylvania. During the suicide attacks, almost 3,000 people were killed.

After the attacks, many Muslims around the world spoke out against these terrorist actions. Despite the strong condemnation, some people felt Islam as a whole was to blame. A number of American Muslims were attacked verbally and physically, and mosques became the target of vandalism and graffiti.

Many conflicts between Muslims and other groups in the Middle East have centered on Israel and the issue of establishing an independent Palestinian state. Numerous terrorist attacks and suicide bombings have plagued Israel over the years, and have been met with equally violent reprisals by the Israeli armed forces. In 2002, there was an average of five terrorist attacks in Israel each month. Palestinians hope for an independent state, while Israelis need to be assured of their future safety.

In the summer of 2006, Israel withdrew from the Gaza Strip, leaving the Palestinians in charge. However, continuing conflicts between Israel and the Palestinians caused Israel to sometimes seal off these areas, limiting the Palestinians' ability to control their territory. In June 2007, a civil war between Palestinian groups Hamas and the Palestine Liberation Organization (PLO) led to Hamas gaining control over Gaza, while the PLO oversaw areas of Palestinian sovereignty in the West Bank.

There has also been division within Muslim nations themselves. Moderate, progressive Muslims have encountered heavy opposition from more traditional, conservative groups, and the more extreme radical Islamist groups. Conservative Muslims worry that Western influences will weaken and erase the traditions that have persisted in Islamic countries for centuries. Muslim women who speak out for equality are jailed in some countries, as are students who try to introduce Western ideas of free speech and democracy.

This Muslim family in Cedar Rapids, Iowa, shares in a feast at their mosque. There are about 6 million Muslims in the United States.

Some of the most radical Muslim groups, referred to as *Islamists*, are far from traditional. They reinterpret sharia law in new ways that allow things like suicide bombings or councils of Muslim scholars approving candidates for election (as happens in Iran). These Islamists are not just turning the clock back or wanting to do things the way they were done in the seventh century. They are often reinterpreting the faith in new ways, all in the name of returning to a purer form of Islam. These groups are small in terms of actual numbers. However, they have received more attention than other Muslim groups.

CONTINUED GROWTH

Despite the struggles within Islam, the religion remains strong and vital throughout the world. Islam continues to attract new followers and remains one of the fastest growing religions in the world. As of 2009, there were an estimated 1.35 billion Muslims in the world. That is 20 percent of the world population. Only Christianity has more followers.

Meanwhile, the economic imbalance between Western Europe and many poorer Islamic countries has led to a rise in Muslim immigration into Europe over the past several decades. Most Europeans value a secular society, in which religion does not play a dominant role. These secular values have clashed with the more conservative beliefs of many Muslim immigrants, sometimes creating tensions within immigrant Muslim communities.

Yet for many Muslims, their religion forms only part of their identity. Like other peoples, they greatly value their individual nationalities and ethnicities. These factors influence how a Muslim chooses to pratice his or her faith, which explains why Muslim groups can vary so much in different regions. Linking each community, however, is a rich history and culture that have significantly impacted the world and continue to have an influence today.

TIME LINE

570	Muhammad, the founder of Islam, is born in Mecca.
632	Muhammad dies in Medina. Abu Bakr becomes the first caliph of the Islamic Empire.
632–661	The era of the first four caliphs, the so-called "rightly guided caliphs": Abu Bakr, Umar, Uthman, and Ali.
633–647	The Muslims conquer Syria and Iraq.
639–642	The Muslims attack and eventually take control of Egypt.
637–651	The Muslims conquer Persia.
653	An official version of the Quran, the Muslim sacred text, is assembled.
661	Muawiya becomes caliph, founding the Umayyad dynasty. Damascus becomes the capital. A number of Muslims, including Kharijite groups and followers of Ali (early Shiites), refuse to recognize Umayyad authority.
680	The Second Civil War breaks out when descendants of two rival caliphs, Ali and Muawiya, battle for control. Husayn (the son of Ali) is killed at Karbala. The split between Shiites and Sunnis becomes permanent.
685–691	The Dome of the Rock mosque is built in Jerusalem by Caliph Abd al-Malik.
696	Arabic becomes the official language of the empire.
705–720	The Muslims begin conquest of Central Asia, India, and Spain.
732	Charles Martel defeats the Muslims at the Battle of Tours in France.
747–750	The Abbasid revolution overthrows Caliph Marwan II and establishes the Abbasid dynasty.
756	Abd al-Rahman establishes the Umayyad emirate of Cordoba in Spain.
762	The city of Baghdad is founded.
786–809	The caliphate of Harun al-Rashid marks the height of Abbasid power.
830	Caliph al-Mamun establishes the Bayt al-Hikma (House of Wisdom) in Baghdad to translate classical Greek and Persian texts into Arabic.
909	The Fatimid caliphate takes control of North Africa and, in 969, Egypt. Cairo becomes its capital.
945	The Buyids take control of Baghdad, leaving the Abbasid caliphs as figureheads.
1031	The Umayyad dynasty in Spain is destroyed. Islamic Spain splits into many small, weaker states.
1055	The Seljuk Turks conquer Baghdad.

1071	The Seljuks defeat the Byzantine army at the Battle of Manzikert, opening the Anatolian Peninsula (modern Turkey) to Muslim conquest.
1085–1266	The Muslims lose all of Spain except Granada.
1092	Seljuk sultan Malik Shah and Vizier Nizam al-Mulk die. The Seljuk dynasty divides into a number of minor kingdoms.
1096	The First Crusade is launched by Europeans to take control of the Holy Lands (today's Israel) from the Muslims.
1099	European crusaders take control of Jerusalem.
1171	Saladin conquers Egypt and eliminates the Fatimid dynasty.
1187	Saladin retakes Jerusalem from the crusaders.
1218–1221	Mongol invaders from the east take over Persia and in 1258 take control of Baghdad, bringing an end to the Islamic Empire.
1260	The Mamluks defeat the Mongols at the Battle of Ayn Jalut, protecting Palestine, Arabia, and Egypt from Mongol conquest.
1326	The Ottoman Turkish state establishes its first capital in Bursa.
1453	The Ottoman conquest of Constantinople ends the Byzantine Empire.
1492	Granada, the last Muslim stronghold in Spain, is defeated by the army of Catholic king and queen Ferdinand and Isabella. By 1500, Muslims are ordered to convert or leave.
1516–1517	The Ottomans conquer Syria and Egypt.

GLOSSARY

alliance a friendship or bond between groups of people

archery shooting with a bow and arrow

architect a person who designs buildings

architecture the way buildings are designed and built

bureaucracy an administrative system with many layers and functions in which most of the important decisions are made by appointed officials, called bureaucrats

caliph the chief Muslim government and religious ruler, considered to be the successor of Muhammad

calligraphy the art of elegant, ornamental writing

concubine a woman who is supported by a man and lives with him without being legally married to him

caravan a group of people traveling together, often traders

cavalry soldiers who fight on horseback

city-state a city that, along with its surrounding territory, forms an independent state

clan a group of close-knit families

commerce the activity of buying and selling goods

courtier a person who lives at the royal court as a friend or advisor to the ruler

crusaders Europeans who went on the Crusades

Crusades military expeditions made by Europeans in the 11th, 12th, and 13th centuries to capture the Holy Land from the Muslims

descendants relatives who trace their roots back to one person

dowry property or money brought by a bride or groom to their marriage

dynasty a family that keeps control of a government over many generations, with rule often passed from a parent to a child

fertile able to easily grow (for plants) or have offspring (for animals and people)

garrison town a town that has soldiers permanently stationed in it

Hadith collection of short reports about what the prophet Muhammad said or did. Individual reports are called *hadith*.

hajj a religious pilgrimage to Mecca

harem a group of women, usually relatives including multiple wives, who lived in a secluded part of the house

idol an image of a god

incense a substance burned for its sweet smell

infantry soldiers who fight on foot

irrigation bringing water to the fields to help crops grow

jihad a Muslim holy war

lance a weapon with a hard point mounted on a wooden pole

martyr a person who is killed because of their religious or other beliefs

mihrab niche in a mosque indicating the direction of Mecca

missionary someone sent to promote his or her religion in a foreign country

monotheism the worship of one god

mosaic pictures made with pieces of colored tile

mosque a Muslim place of worship

nomad a person with no permanent home who wanders from place to place

oasis an area in the desert that has water and growing plants

oral tradition remembering history by telling stories

philosopher a person who thinks about the meaning of life and how to lead a better life; in ancient times, many philosophers were also scientists

philosophy the study of the nature of the world

pilgrimage a journey to a special scared place; people who take such a journey are called pilgrims

polygamy having more than one wife

polytheism worshipping more than one god

prophet a person who is considered to be an inspired teacher or someone who declares the message of God

qibla direction of Mecca

reign the period during which a particular ruler rules

reservoir a natural or artificial lake used to supply water

ritual a ceremony carried out according to religious laws and customs

sharia Islamic moral and legal codes

siege cutting off a town or fort from the outside so it cannot receive supplies and the citizens cannot escape

succession passing on the family's rank; the verb is to succeed

successor a person who comes after another and inherits or continues in the offices they held

textiles cloth, or the items made from cloth

theocracy a government in which religious rulers govern in the name of God

tunic a long, loose garment, somewhat like a shirt except it usually reaches to the wearer's knees or below

umma the worldwide community of Muslims

vizier a top-level administrator who is knowledgeable in literature, writing, management, taxation, and many other areas

BIBLIOGRAPHY

"The Largest Muslim Communities." Adherents. com. Available online. URL: http://www.adherents. com/largecom/com_islam.html. Accessed January 27, 2005.

Ahmed, Akbar S. *From Samarkand to Stornoway: Living Islam.* New York: Facts On File, 1994.

Armstrong, Karen. *Islam: A Short History.* New York: Random House, 2000.

Averröes. "Kitab fasl al-maqal (On the harmony of religions and philosophy)." Medieval Sourcebook. Available online. URL: http://www.fordham.edu/ halsall/source/1190averroes.html#Introduction. Accessed March 12, 2008.

Beverley, James A. *Islamic Faith in Americ*a, New York: Facts On File, 2003.

"The Mosque in America: A National Portrait." Council on American-Islamic Relations. Available online. URL: http://www.cair-net.org/mosquereport/ Masjid_Study_Project_2000_Report.pdf. Accessed April 26, 2005.

De Expugatione Terrae Sanctae per Saladinum (The capture of the Holy Land by Saladin). Brundage, James A., translator. *The Crusades: A Documentary Survey.* Milwaukee, Wisc.: Marquette University Press, 1962. Available online. "The Capture of Jerusalem by Saladin, 1187." Medieval Sourcebook. URL: http://www.fordham.edu/halsall/source/1187saladin. html. Accessed March 21, 2008.

Esposito, John L., Ed. *The Oxford History of Islam.* New York: Oxford University Press, 1999.

Farah, Caesar E. *Islam.* New York: Barron's Educational Series, 2000.

FitzGerald, Edward, translator. *Rubaiyat of Omar Khayyam.* London: Penguin Books, 1985.

Fulcher of Chartres. "Gesta Francorum Jerusalem Expugnantium." Thatcher, Oliver J., and Edgar Holmes, editors. *A Source Book for Medieval History,* New York: Charles Scribner and Sons, 1905. Available online. "Urban II: Speech at Council of Clermont, 1095, Five versions of the Speech." Medieval Sourcebook. URL: http://www.fordham.edu/ halsall/source/urban2-5vers.html. Accessed March 25, 2008.

Glassé, Cyril. *The Concise Encyclopedia of Islam.* New York: HarperCollins, 1991.

Gordon, Matthew S. *Islam: Origins, Practices, Holy Texts, Sacred Persons, Sacred Places.* New York: Oxford University Press, 2002.

"American Religious Identification Survey 2001." Graduate Center of the City University of New York. Available online. URL: http://www.gc.cuny.edu/ faculty/research_studies.htm#aris_1. Accessed March 1, 2005.

Grupper, Jonathan. *Islam: Empire of Faith* (DVD). Gardner Films, 2000.

"The Hanged Poems." *Medieval Islamic Sourcebook: Pre 622.* Available online. URL: http://www.fordham. edu/halsall/source/640hangedpoems.html. Accessed April 1, 2008.

Hitti, Philip K. *The Arabs: A Short History.* Washington, D.C.: Regnery Publishing, 1996.

Horne, Charles F. *The Sacred Books and Early Literature of the East.* New York: Parke, Austin & Lipscomb, 1917. Available online. "Address to His Troops by Tariq ibn-Ziyad." WikiSource: Military Texts. URL: http://en.wikisource.org/wiki/ Tariq%27s_Address_to_his_Troops. Accessed March 25, 2008.

———. *The Sacred Books and Early Literature of the East.* New York: Parke, Austin & Lipscomb, 1917. Available online. "Al Biruni (973-1048 CE): The Existing Monuments or Chronology, c. 1030 CE." Medieval Sourcebook. URL: http://www.fordham. edu/halsall/source/1030al-biruni1.html. Accessed March 25, 2008.

Hourani, Albert. *A History of the Arab Peoples.* Cambridge, Mass.: The Belknap Press of Harvard University Press, 1991.

Ibn Ishaq. "Selections from the Life of Muhammad." Medieval Sourcebook. Available online. URL: http://www.fordham.edu/halsall/source/muhammadi-sira.html. Accessed March 6, 2008.

Jandora, John Walter. *Militarism in Arab Society: An Historiographical and Bibliographical Sourcebook.* Westport, Conn.: Greenwood, 1997.

Lewis, Bernard. *The Arabs in History.* New York: Oxford University Press, 2002.

——. *A Middle East Mosaic: Fragments of Life, Letters, and History.* New York: Random House: 2000.

——. *The Middle East: A Brief History of the Last 2,000 Years.* New York: Scribner, 1995.

——. *The Muslim Discovery of Europe.* New York: W.W. Norton & Co., 2001.

Lewis, Brenda. Ralph, editor. *Great Civilizations.* Bath, U.K.: Paragon Publishing, 1999.

"Manumission of Slaves, Translation of Sahih Bukhari, Volume 3, Book 46, Number 694." University of Southern California USC-MSA Compendium of Muslim Texts. Available online. URL: http://www.usc.edu/dept/MSA/fundamentals/hadithsunnah/bukhari/046.sbt.html#003.046.702. Accessed March 3, 2008.

"al-Mutanabbi: The Greatest of Classical Arab Poets." The Arab Washingtonian. Available online. URL: http://www.arabwashingtonian.org/english/article.php?issue=10&articleID=255. Accessed March 29, 2008.

Newby, Gordon D. *A Concise Encyclopedia of Islam.* Oxford, U.K.: Oneworld Publications, 2002.

Nizam al-Mulk. "On the Courtiers and Familiars of Kings, from Treatise on the Art of Government, translated by Reuben Levy, M.A., 1929." Medieval Sourcebook. Available online. URL: http://www.fordham.edu/halsall/source/nizam-courtiers.html. Accessed April 28, 2004.

"OIC in Brief." Organization of the Islamic Conference. Available online. URL: http://www.oicun.org/categories/The-OIC/About-OIC/OIC-in-brief/. Accessed April 2, 1008.

"Pact of Umar, 7th Century." Medieval Sourcebook. Available online. URL: http://www.fordham.edu/halsall/source/pact-umar.html. Accessed March 5, 2008.

Perry, Charles, translator. "An Anonymous Andalusian Cookbook of the 13th Century," Recreational Medievalism. Available online. URL: http://www.daviddfriedman.com/Medieval/Cookbooks/Andalusian/andalusian1.htm#Heading6. Accessed March 6, 2008.

Racy, A. J. "Arab Music," Turath.org. Available online. URL: http://www.turath.org. Accessed January 10, 2005.

Renard, John. *Responses to 101 Questions on Islam.* New York: Paulist Press, 1998.

——. *Windows on the House of Islam: Muslim Sources on Spirituality and Religious Life.* Berkeley, Calif.: University of California Press, 1998.

Robinson, Francis, editor. *Islamic World.* New York: Cambridge University Press, 1996.

Savage-Smith, Emilie. "Islamic Culture and the Medical Arts," National Library of Medicine. Available online. URL: http://www.nlm.nih.gov/exhibition/islamic_medical/islamic_00.html. Accessed April 15, 2005.

Stewart, Desmond. *Early Islam.* New York: Time Inc., 1967.

Suhufi, Sayyid Muhammad. *Lessons from Islam.* Karachi, Pakistan: Prima Printers, 1999.

Swisher, Clarice, editor. *The Spread of Islam.* San Diego, Calif.: Greenhaven Press, 1999.

Time-Life Books. *What Life Was Like in the Lands of the Prophet.* Alexandria, Va.: Time-Life, 1999.

Watt, W. Montgomery. *Muhammad: Prophet and Statesman.* Oxford, U.K.: Oxford University Press, 1961.

"World Scripture—Traces of God's Existence." Unification.net. Available online. URL: http://www.unification.net/ws/theme001.htm. Accessed April 1, 2008.

Yazid, "To My Father." In "Arabic Poetry, Selections." Then Again. . . Primary Source. Available online. URL: http://www.thenagain.info/Classes/Sources/ArabPoetry.html. Accessed March 28, 2008.

FURTHER RESOURCES

BOOKS

Beshore, George. *Science in Early Islamic Culture* (London: Franklin Watts, 1998)

This book begins with the 600s and describes early medical advances, the development of Arabic numerals, and other topics in the history of science. It looks at the historical and cultural background of the empire and the parts they played in the development of science. Some individual scientists are highlighted and the actual processes used by scientists are explained in detail. Many photographs, reproductions, and drawings illustrate the text.

DK Publishing. *Eyewitness Islam* (New York: DK Publishing, 2005)

This book covers the history of the Islamic Empire and the practice of Islam. Using photos, art, and artifacts left behind, it looks at early Arabia, Muhammad, the Quran, mosques, the Five Pillars of Islam, Islamic culture, the Crusades, arms and armor, Islam in Spain, North Africa and Asia, clothing and jewelry, Islamic festivals, and more.

Editors of Time-Life Books. *What Life Was Like in the Lands of the Prophet* (New York: Time-Life Inc., 1999)

A colorful look at the Islamic world from 570 to 1405. Beautiful illustrations, maps, and interesting boxes are included. The first part covers the life of Muhammad. The second part deals with the conquests of the Islamic Empire. The last part looks at the everyday lives of doctors and tradesmen.

Ford, Nick. *Jerusalem Under Muslim Rule in the Eleventh Century* (New York: Rosen Publishing Group, 2004)

In the early 11th century, just before the First Crusade, Jerusalem was ruled by a Muslim government. This book looks at what it was like for the Christians who lived under Muslim rule. It details the government and culture of the Middle East under Islamic rulers.

Nicolle, David. *Historical Atlas of the Islamic World* (New York: Checkmark Books, 2005)

The book starts with the culture of pre-Islamic Arabia and its contacts with its neighbors. It continues through the period of the early caliphs and on into the various ruling dynasties and peoples that marked Islam. It examines such early dynasties as the Umayyads and the Abbasids, as well as the conquerors who came after the fall of the Islamic Empire. The author points out the ways in which Islamic culture absorbed and changed ideas from conquered peoples and from later conquerors. The book also looks at the Muslims in Spain, India, sub-Saharan Africa, and Russia, as well as Muslim advances in geography, astronomy, and various arts.

Robinson, Francis, editor. *The Cambridge Illustrated History of the Islamic World* (New York: Cambridge University Press, 1999)

Facts about Islam's history and practice are presented, along with its economic, social, and intellectual structures. They authors discuss the importance in Islamic culture of commerce, literacy and learning, and art. They also take on current issues, such as the role of religious and political fundamentalism, the effects of immigration and conquest, and the roots of current crises in the Middle East, Bosnia, and the Persian Gulf. Throughout, emphasis is placed on the interaction between Islam and the West. There are excellent graphics and maps, and boxes throughout provide more depth on key issues.

DVDS

Islam: Empire of Faith (PBS Paramount, 2005)

This is the DVD of the three-part PBS documentary that charts the history of Islam from its beginnings in Mecca and Medina in the seventh century to the Ottoman Empire 1,000 years later. Reenacted and actual scenes make the beginnings of the Islamic Empire come to life. The DVD shows the riches of Islamic culture and the vital role played by Islam in preserving and building on ancient wisdom from East and West. The faith itself is clearly explained, and interviews with historians and religious scholars discuss important points.

WEB SITES

History for Kids: Medieval Islam

www.historyforkids.org/learn/islam/index.htm

A big site with lots of pictures and information about history, everyday life, economics, art, architecture, and science. Includes maps, crafts, and projects to do.

Islam: Empire of Faith

www.pbs.org/empires/islam

A companion site to the public television program (and video) of the same name. The site contains information about the faith, culture, and innovations of the Islamic Empire, and profiles of important figures.

Islamic Art at the Los Angeles County Museum of Art

www.lacma.org/islamic_art/eip.htm

The Islamic art collection of this museum includes a wide variety of objects, including statues, textiles, calligraphy, illuminations, decorated household objects, boxes, jars, and more. There are lots of photos. The objects are divided into historical periods, with an essay about each period. There are also many photos of Islamic architecture.

Islamic Arts and Architecture Organization

www.islamicart.com/index.html

This site, sponsored by the Islamic Arts and Architecture Organization, has articles about and pictures and descriptions of Islamic architecture, calligraphy, rugs, and coins. It also includes a history of the Islamic Empire, greeting cards, downloads, a museum directory and interesting links to other sites.

Islamic Culture and the Medical Arts

www.nlm.nihgov/exhibition/islamic_medical/islamic_00.html

This site from the National Library of Medicine takes a tour of a virtual museum exhibit about the many important contributions Islamic doctors have made to medicine. It includes original drawings and pages from ancient medical texts.

LookLex Encyclopaedia

www.lexicorient.com/e.o/

An encyclopedia of geographical, historical, and current information on the nations of the Middle East and North Africa. It offers a search by place name, person, or country.

Medieval Islamic Cultures

www.sfusd.k12.ca.us/schwww/sch618/Islam_New_Main.html

A wide variety of cultural topics are covered here, including some unusual ones. There is information on how animals were used in the Islamic Empire, sports and recreation, farming and food, clothing, and festivals and entertainment. More typical topics, such as education, literature, art, warfare, and the roles of women and family are also discussed. The text is specifically for middle school students, and includes many illustrations, links to other pages, and original source material that is fully explained.

Muslim Heritage

www.muslimheritage.com

This site presents a wide overview of the contributions of Muslim scientists, writers, and artists. It includes an excellent interactive timeline of Islamic history. There is also an interactive map that shows Muslim monuments, discoveries, and personalities all around the world.

PICTURE CREDITS

Page

6: The Art Archive/Turkish and Islamic Art Museum Istanbul/Alfredo Dagli Orti

11: Erich Lessing/Art Resource, NY

12: Erich Lessing/Art Resource, NY

16: The New York Public Library/Art Resource, NY

19: Ayazad/Shutterstock

23: Erich Lessing/Art Resource, NY

25: © The Metropolitan Museum of Art/Art Resource, NY

34: Holger Mette/Shutterstock

40: Werner Forman/Art Resource, NY

42: Louvre, Paris, France/Peter Willi/The Bridgeman Art Library

44: Erich Lessing/Art Resource, NY

48: Shutterlist/Shutterstock

49: Elias H. Debbas II/Shutterstock

52: Erich Lessing/Art Resource, NY

54: Art Resource, NY

58: Umayyad Mosque, Damascus, Syria/The Bridgeman Art Library

65: Erich Lessing, Art Resource, NY

67: Art Resource, NY

69: © The Metropolitan Museum of Art/Art Resource, NY

72: © Nik Wheeler/CORBIS

75: Giraudon/The Bridgeman Art Library International

79: The Art Archive/Bibliothèque Nationale Paris

84: Werner Forman/Art Resource, NY

88: The Art Archive/Bodleian Library Oxford/MS. Ouseley Add 24 folio 55v

92: Bibliotheque Nationale, Paris, France/Archives Charmet/The Bridgeman Art Library International

94: Private Collection/The Bridgeman Art Library International

98: Werner Forman/Art Resource, NY

102: Réunion des Musées Nationaux/Art Resource, NY

105: Vanni/Art Resource, NY

113: Erich Lessing/Art Resource, NY

120: Dita Alangkara/AP Images

124: Karim Kadim/AP Images

128: Kevin Wolf/AP Images

INDEX

A

abacus 118
Abbas, al- 41
Abbasah 62
Abbasid dynasty **41–43**, *75*, **90–91**, 129*c*
  Africa and 50
  class system 64
  clothing 85–86
  culture 43–44, 85, 90, 95, 103, 108
  food and diet 83, 92
  government and politics 45–46, 47, 50, 52, **61–63**, 64
  money and banking 80
  religion and beliefs 43, 45, 62, 80
  trade and commerce 79
Abd al-Malik ibn Marwan 37–38, 129*c*
Abd al-Rahman I 41, 47, 77, 107, 129*c*
Abd al-Rahman II 103
Abd al-Rahman III *42*, 47
Abraham 11, 22, 26, 66, 93
Abu al-Abbas al-Saffah 41, 42–43
Abu Bakr *17*, 21, 26, 27–29, 123, 129*c*
Abu Hanafi 71
Abul Wafa 116
Abu Nuwas 98
Abu Talib 17
adab 99
Adam 11, 19, 22, 66
Afghanistan 8, 13, 29, 122, 125
Africa 14, 38, 39*m*, 68–69, 71, 95, 121. *See also* North Africa; specific country
  trade and 78, 79
  violence and 21, 125
afterlife 20, 30, 92
Aghlabids 50, 51
agriculture 10, 43, 76. *See also* food
Ahmad ibn Hanbal 71
Aisha 33
Aladdin (movie) 13
alcachofa 49
alchemy 109, 119
alcohol. *See* drugs and alcohol
aldea 49
Alexandria 31, 105–106
Alexios I Komnenos 53
algebra 109, 118
Algeria 38, 50, 125
Alhambra, the *45*, 47, 48, 49
Alhazen. *See* Ibn al-Haytham
Ali *17*, 27, 33, 36, 50, 122, 129*c*

Ali Baba (fictional character) 100
aljibe 49
Allah 11, 25, 55, 68, 115. *See also* Hadith; mosques; Quran
  art and 101, 105
  Hagar and the Zamzam well 93
"Allahu Akbar!" 24, 55
alliances 7, 20, 21, 53, 131*g*
Almohads 48
Almoravids 47–48
Amin, al- 17, 45
Anatolia *54*, 130*c*
Andalusia 41, 48, 81, 104
anesthesia 113, 114–115
animals 29, 30, 81, 90, 92. *See also* specific animal
animism 11, 22, 26
Aqsa Mosque 106–107
arabesque 49, 84
Arabia 11, 13, 28, 56, 60, 96, 100, 130*c*
Arabian coffee 14
Arabian Peninsula 8–10, 14, 28–29, 68, 71
  geography and climate 7, 9, 11, 29, 30
  invasions of 12, 30–31
Arabica coffee 14
Arabic language 7, 9, 12–13, 14, 51, 63, 123. *See also* translations
  official language 73, 95, 129*c*
  Spanish Inquisition and 48, 49, 130*c*
Arabic numerals 118, 119
Arabs 9, 13–14, 31–32, 74. *See also* Bedouins; tribes
  culture 95, 101
  goods produced 10–11
  non-Arabs and 63, 64–65, 68
archery 17, 131*g*
architecture 49, **105–108**, 131*g*
  Moorish *45, 47, 48, 49,* 77
aristocracy 64
Aristotle 95, 110
Arkan al-Islam 22
army 23–24, 28, 68, 75, 76, 122, 130*c*
  Abbasid dynasty and 62, 63–64, 65
  Umayyad dynasty and 35, 38–40, 60, 63
art **101–102**. *See also* specific type of art
  Allah and 101, 105
  depictions of people in *84*, 101, 107
  destruction of idols in Mecca 24, 25
artisans 77, 81, 98, 105
Asia 8, 13, 36, 39*m*, 40, 71, 78, 86, 129*c*
Asia Minor 8, 121
Assassins 56
astrolabe 114
astronomy 96, 103, 114, **115–117**
Averroës. *See* Ibn Rushd
Avicenna. *See* Ibn Sina
awariyah 80
Ayn Jalut, battle of 130*c*

Ayyubid dynasty 52
Azerbaijan 122
Azhar Mosque, al- *52*
Azhar University, al- 51

B

Babylon 10
backgammon 91
Badr, battle of *23*, 24, 30
Baghdad 50, 51, 71, **74–76**, 86, 123
  culture *67*, 90, 92, 100, 108, 109, 128*c*
  founding of 43, 75, 129*c*
  government and politics 43, 46, 62, *124*
  health and medicine 113, 115
  invasions of 56, 129*c*, 130*c*
  science and technology 109, 116
  trade and commerce *75*, 78, 79, 80
Balkan Peninsula 8
Balkans 121
bancras 109
Bangladesh 13
banking. *See* money and banking
baraka 50
Barbary Coast 38
Barmecides 62
Basra 33, 69, 74
bathhouses 86, 87
Battani, al- 116
battering rams 29, 30
battles *11*, 25, 28, 31, 36, 38. *See also* specific battle
Bayt al-Hikma. *See* House of Wisdom
Bedouins 9–10, 17, 23, 28, 31, 63, 90
  culture 87, 104
  food and diet 81
  housing 83
  jinn and 13
belly dancing 103
Berbers 38, 41, 47–48, 50, 51
Bible, the 11, 22, 26, 66, 93
bin Laden, Osama 125
Biruni, al- 111
Black Stone 11, 18, 19, 26
Bloom, Orlando 50
boats and ships 37, 38, 75, 76, 78, *79,* 117
borax 109
Brahe, Tycho 116
bread 82
Britain. *See* Great Britain
Buhkara 113, 114
buraq 109
bureaucracy 61–63, 131*g*
burial. *See* death and burial
Bursa 130*c*
Buyid dynasty 46, 47, 129*c*
Byzantine Empire 7, 8–9, *11*, 53, 80, 130*c*
  culture 85, 95, 105
  invasions of 12, 29–32, 38–40, 47, 109

C

Cairo 51, *52*, 76, 116, 129*c*
calendars 19, 21, 22, 36, **115–117**
caliphs/caliphate 27, 36, 59–60, 61, 74,
    90–91, 131*g. See also* courtiers; palaces;
    succession; specific caliph or dynasty
  authority of 59
  "protectors" of 63, 64, 68
  royal protocols 50, 60, 61, 91
  sultan vs. 46<\206>47
  support of poetry 98, 99
calligraphy 19, 24, *95*, 101, 131*g*
Camel, battle of the 33
camels 78, 79, 84
  Bedouins and 9, 10, *12*
  warfare and 28, 29, 31, 33, 74, 81
camphor 109
caravans 11, 23–24, 38, 131*g*
  trade and 10, 17–18, 23, 78–79
caravanserai 78
carpets. *See* rugs and carpets
Casablanca 106
Catholic Church 47, 48, 51, 54, 78, 111, 130*c*
cauterization 113
cavalry 28, 131*g*
celebrations and holidays 11, 36, **91–92,**
    103, 117
  fasting 22, 71, 92
Central America 14
Central Asia 13, 36, 40, 122, 129*c*
ceramics 77, 102, 105
Chad 50
chamberlains 61
charity, role of 20, 22, 68, 71
Charlemagne 63
chemistry 112, 119
chess 91
children 24, 37, 66, 68, 69, 74, 88, 90
China 8–9, 13, 49, 54, 78, 79, 82, 117
Chinggis Khan 54–56
Christianity 13, 22, 32, *35*, 65, 111, 128
  Abbasid dynasty and 62, 80
  architecture 105, 107
  Byzantine Empire and 30
  Catholicism 51
  Crusades 50, **52–54,** 55, 130*c*, 131*g*
  Pact of Umar and 66
  "protected minority" 66
  in Spain 48, 49
Chronicon Anglicanum (Ralph of
    Coggeshall) 55
Chronology (Biruni, al-) 111
city-states 47–48, 131*g*
civil wars **32–33,** 37–38, 45, 129*c*
clans 74, 97, 131*g. See also* tribes
class system 60, 62, **64–69.** *See also* spe-
    cific class
climate. *See* geography and climate
clothing 9, 28, 67, **85–86,** 89
  caliphs and 50, 61
  death and burial 92–93
  women and 85, 87–88, 93
coffee 14, 104, 123
coins and currency 35, 61, 80
Commander of the Faithful 29
commerce. *See* trade and commerce
concubines 69, 91, 131*g*
Constantinople 38–40, 109, 130*c*
Copernicus 116

Cordoba *42*, 49, **77–78,** 107, 110, 129*c*
cosmetics 86
courtiers 64, 75, 85, 89, 91, 99, 108, 131*g*
Court of the Lions *45*
Crusades 50, **52–54,** 55, 130*c*, 131*g*
Ctesiphon 31
culture 7–8, 12, 13, 70, 73, 74–78, 95–96,
    128. *See also under* specific region,
    country, city
  spread of through trade 54, 78
currency. *See* coins and currency

D

Daibul 40
daily life **81–86,** 90–91. *See also* prayer
damascened steel 36
Damascus 33, 36, 38, 43, 129*c*
  invasions of 29–30, 31, 74
  Umayyad Mosque *35*, 59, 107
damask 36
dancing 92, 103, 104
Dante Alighieri 77
darbukkah 104
David 32
death and burial *35*, 36, **92–93.** *See also*
    afterlife
decorative arts *11*
denarius 80
dental hygiene 87
descendants 131*g*
desert 9–10, 17, 29, 43
Detroit 14
dhimmis 66–67
dhows 79
Dhu al-Hijja 22, 92, 117
diet. *See* food and diet
diplomacy 18, 21, 23, 25, 26, 35, 63
dirham 80
disease 114, 115
diwans 61, 85
dogs 90
Dome of the Rock 106–107, 129*c*
Dominic (saint) 78
Dorylaeum, battle of *54*
dowries 86, 89, 131*g*
drugs and alcohol 29, 56, 109
  health and medicine 112, 113, 114, 115
  laws regarding 70, 71, 78, 82, 83, 89, 98
dynasties 131*g. See also* caliphs/caliphate;
    specific dynasty

E

Eastern Roman Empire. *See* Byzantine
    Empire
economy 23, 40–41, 42, 66, 128. *See also*
    money and banking; trade and com-
    merce
education 70–71, 89, 90
Egypt 10, 90. *See also* specific city
  Abbasid dynasty and 52
  Byzantine Empire 8, 29
  culture 100, 102–103, 105–106, 116
  Fatimid dynasty and 50–52
  government and politics 125
  invasions of 29, 129*c*, 130*c*
  laws 70, 71
  Mamluk dynasty 69
  Umayyad dynasty 43

Eid al-Adha 91–92
Eid al-Fitr 92
elephants 31, 63
elixir 109
emirs 47, 77
England 28
entertainment 89–90, 91
Ethiopia 14, 21
Euclid 95
eunuchs 91
Euphrates River 30
Europe 29, 85, 121, 128, 130*c. See also*
    Crusades; specific country
  culture 8, 49, 54, 77, 81, 91, 111
  food and diet 14
  health and medicine 86, 111, 112, 114
  invasions of 32, 36, 38, 39*m*, 40
  music 103, 104
  science and technology 96, 118, 119
  trade and commerce 49, 78, 80, 82, 87

F

falafel 82
family life 64, 74, 83, **86–90,** 92, *128. See
    also* children; clans; dynasties; mar-
    riage; tribes
faqih/fuqaha 70, 122
Farewell Pilgrimage (hajj) 25–26
farming 10, 43. *See also* agriculture; food
fasting 22, 71, 92
Fatima al-Zahraa 18, 27, 50, *52*
Fatimid dynasty **50–52,** 76, 92, 129*c*, 130*c*
Ferdinand (king of Aragon) 48, 130*c*
Ferdinand of Castile 78
fertile 9, 10, 30, 75, 131*g*
festivals. *See* celebrations and holidays
finance 80
"finger reckoning" 118
fiqh 70
First Crusade 53, 130*c*
fitna 32–33
Five Pillars of Islam 22, 71
flamenco music 104
folk tales 13, 99, 100–101
food and diet 22, 43, 71, 79, **81–83,** 91. *See
    also* agriculture; laws
  fasting 22, 71, 92
  laws regarding 70, 71, 78, 82, 83, 89, 98
  trade and 14, 49, 82
France 40, 51, 53, 63, 103, 121, 129*c*
frankincense 10–11
Frederick II (king of Sicily) 51
Fulcher of Chartres 53
fundamentalism *124,* 125, **127–128**
furniture 83, *84,* 85, 86
Fustat 76

G

Gabriel 18
Galen 96, 111, 112
games 91
garrison towns **73–78,** 76, 131*g*
Gaza Strip 127
Geber. *See* Ibn Hayyan
Genghis Khan. *See* Chinggis Khan
genies 13
geography and climate 41, 43, 111, **117**
  Arabian Peninsula 7, 9, 11, 29, 30

Germany 40, 77
Gibraltar, Straight of 41
Giralda Tower 49
God 11, 12, 13, 18, 22. *See also* Allah
gold 31, 32, 76
government and politics 21, 23, 29, 121,
    128. *See also* caliphs/caliphate; court-
    iers; governors; specific country or
    dynasty
  city-states 47–48
  diplomacy 18, 21, 23, 25, 26, 35, 63
  garrison towns *73–78*, *76*, 131*g*
  Quraysh and 12, 25
  Taliban 29
  theocracy 59, 122, 132*g*
governors 35, 45–46, 50, 60, 63
Granada *45*, 47, *48*, 49, 130*c*
Grand Mosque (Mecca) *19*
Great Britain 28, 55, 121
Great Mosque at Samarra 106
Great Mosque (Cordoba) 107
Great Mosque (Damascus) 107
Greece 95–96, 103, 108–109, 110, 111, 115,
    118. *See also* translations
Guadalete, battle of 37
guitars 103, 104

H

Hadi, al- 90
Hadith 68, *69*–70, 90, 97, 131*g*
Hagar 93
hair 86
hajj *19*, 22, 25–26, 93, 131*g*
halal 83
Hamas 127
hammamat 87
Hanafi law school 71
Hanbali law school 71
Hanged Poems 97
haram 71
harems 19, 51, 87, 91, 108, 131*g*
harras 82
Hartford Seminary 14
Harun al-Rashid 45, 62, 63, 75, 76, 83–84,
    95, 129*c*
Hashemite clan 17
hashish 56
hashshash 56
Hassan II Mosque 106
Haydar Khana Mosque *75*
health and medicine 86, 87, 93, 95–96,
    111–114, 115
henna 86
hijab 85, 87–88, 93
Hijaz 11
Hijra 21, 30, 116
Hindus 95, 112, 118, 119
Hippocrates 96, 111
Hira, Mount 18
historians/history 53, 55, 96, 104
  oral tradition 96, 97, 100, 131*g*
holidays. *See* celebrations and holidays
Holy Land 52–54, 130*c*
Holy Mosque 26
holy wars. *See* jihad
Homer 96
horses 41, 60, 67, 84
  horsemanship 17, 24, 91
  warfare and 24, 28, 29, 31, 54, 74, 81

hospitals 113, 115
House of Wisdom 109, 129*c*
housing 49, 77, **83–85**. *See also* furniture;
    palaces
howdahs 30
Hubal 11
Hülegü 55, 56
hummus 82
Hunayn ibn Ishaq 113
hunting 91
Husayn, al- 36, 37, 129*c*
Hussein, Saddam 124
hygiene 83, 86, 87, 112, 115

I

Iberian Peninsula 37, 38, 49
Ibn Aqil *73*
Ibn al-Haytham 113
Ibn Hayyan 119
Ibn Ishaq 20, 99
Ibn Khaldun 38
Ibn al-Khatib 115
Ibn al-Muqaffaa 99–100
Ibn Rushd 110–111
Ibn Sina 113–114
Ibn al-Zubayr, Abdullah 37–38
Ibrahim ibn al-Aghlab 50
Ibrahim ibn al-Mahdi 81–82
idols 20–21, 22, 24, 25, 67, 131*g*
ijma 70
iksir, al- 109
illuminated manuscripts 101, 102
iman 36, 106
incense 10–11, 131*g*
India 7, 13, 43, 71
  culture *84*, 86, 91, 99–100, 102
  geography and climate 111, 117
  invasions of 31, 129*c*
  laws 70, 71
  science and technology 115, 119
  trade and commerce 76, 78, 79
Indian Ocean 9
Indonesia 13, 70, *121*, 122
Indus River Valley 40
infantry 28, 131*g*
Inquisition, Spanish 48, 49, 130*c*
instruments, musical **103–104**, *105*
Iran 8, 40, 46. *See also* specific city
  culture 86, 92
  government and politics 13, 122,
    124–125, 128, 132*g*
  invasions of 29, 31, 33, 54
  laws 70
  religion and beliefs 13, 56, 70
  science and technology 116
Iraq 8, 28, 30, 36, **74–76**. *See also* specific
    city
  culture 76, *113*
  government and politics 13, 37, 74,
    124–125
  invasions of 29, 54–55, 69, 121,
    129*c*
  laws 70, 71
  religion and beliefs 13, 37, 124–125
Iraq War 124–125
irrigation 10, 43, 76, 131*g*
Isaac 26
Isabella (queen of Castile) 48, 130*c*
Ishmael 26, 93

Islam 23, 32. *See also* jihad; Kaaba;
    Muslims; sacred texts; Shiites; Sunnis
  Christianity and 48, 49, 66, 125, 130*c*
  conversions to 12–13, 21, 25, 33, 62–63,
    76, 121–122
    Ali 27, 38
    Barmecides 62
    Berbers 38, 50
    dhimmis 67
    al-Mahdi 50
    mawali 64–65
    Muhammad 35
  dietary laws 70, 71, 78, 82, 83, 89, 98
  Five Pillars of 22, 71
  founding of 7–8, 12–13, 20, 21
  growth of 12, 13–14, 25, 122, 128
  Hijra 21, 30, 116
  split of 27, 33, 129*c*
  tribes and 27
Islamic Empire 43, 54–56, 130*c*. *See also*
  caliphs/caliphate; specific dynasty
  civil wars **32–33**, 37–38, 45, 129*c*
  founding of 7–8
  growth of 7, 39*m*, 59, 60, 64, 126*m*, 128
  legacy of **13–15**, 121–122, 126*m*
Islamists 128
isnad 97
Israel 13, 53, 127, 130*c*
Italy 14, 40, 82, 87
ivory *42*

J

Jabal Tariq. *See* Gibraltar, Straight of
jabr, al- 109, 118
Jafar 62
Jakarta *121*
Jamaat al-Islamiyya 125
Jawsaq Palace 108
Jerusalem 32, 106, 107, 129*c*
  Crusades and 50, **52–54**, 55, 130*c*, 131*g*
Jesus 11, 22, 32
Jews 12, 24, 26, 32, 48, 62, 66, 80
  Crusades and 52, 53
  culture 65, 95, 119
jihad 22, 30–31, 38, 121, 125, 131*g*
jinn 13
John the Baptist *35*
Judaism 12, 22, 23, 32, 65, 111

K

Kaaba *7*, 21, 25, 97
  Black Stone 11, 18, 19, 26
  care and maintenance of 12, 18
  origins of 11, *19*
  Quraysh and 18, 21
Kadisiya 30
Kaffa 14
kafur 109
Kalila and Dimna 99
Karbala 36
Khadija 17–18, 87
Khalid ibn al-Walid 28–29, 107
khamr 83
Kharijites 33, 50, 71, 78, 129*c*
Khurasan 45–46
Khwarizmi, al- 119
kimiya, al- 109
Kindi, al- 119

Kingdom of Heaven (movie) 50
Kitab al-Hawi fi al-tibb (Razi) 112
Kitab al-Hind (Biruni, al-) 111
Koran. *See* Quran
Kufa 33, *73*, 74
kuhl, al- 109

L

lance 28, 131*g*
language and writing 49, 97–98, 101, 118, 123. *See also* Arabic language; calligraphy; literature; translations
laws 20, 23, 29, 59, **69–71,** 97, 106
   class system and 67
   dietary 70, 71, 78, 82, 83, 89, 98
   modern 121–122, 125, 128
   origins of 7–8, 12, 18
Lebanon 53
libraries 76, 90, 98
Libya 50
literature 13, 20, *23*, 48, 77, 81, 91, **96–101.** *See also* sacred texts
Los Angeles 14
lutes 104

M

madhhabs 70
madinat al-nabi 21
Madinat al-Salam 75. *See also* Baghdad
Madinat al-Zahra 47
madrasas 90
Magians 111
Mahdi, al- 50, 90
Mahdiyah 50
mail (clothing) 28
Mali 50
Malik ibn Anas 71
Maliki law school 71
Malik Shah 130*c*
Mamluks 52, 69, 130*c*
Mamun, al- 45, 81, 91, 109, 129*c*
Mansur, al- 43, 75, 99
manumission 68
manuscripts *95*, 98, 101, 102, *113*
Manzikert, battle of 130*c*
mapmaking 117
maqama 100–101
Maraghah 116
marriage 9, 20, 62, 86–87, 91. *See also* harems
   non-Arabs and 64, 65, 68
Martel, Charles 40, 63, 129*c*
martyrs 30, 36, 93, 125, 131*g*
Marwa, Mount 93
Marwan II 129*c*
Mary 22
Massoud, Ghassan 50
mathematics 95, 109, **117–119**
matrah 85
mattresses 83, 85, 123
mawala 64
mawali 64–66
Maylasia 122
Mecca **11–13,** *19,* 29, 32, 67, 71, 129*c. See also* Kaaba; pilgrimage; Quraysh
   culture 97, 98
   destruction of idols in 24, 25
   invasions of 23–25, 30, 37–38

prayer and 26, 51, 106
Zamzan well 92, 93
mediator 21
mediation. *See* health and medicine
Medina 21, 24–25, 27, 29, 33, 71, 105. *See also* Yathrib
Medinian period 21
Mediterranean Revival 77
men **85–86,** 89–90, 106
Mesopotamia 28
Messina *40*
Middle Ages 8, 29
Middle East 49, 121, 127. *See also* specific country
   battle for control of *11*
   Crusades and 52–53
   culture 105
   food and diet 14, 82
   health and medicine 87, 105
   invasions of 8, 9, 29
mihbaj 104
mihrab 26, 84, 106, 107, 131*g*
minbar 106
minarets 105–106, 107
missionaries 131*g*
Mohammed VI (king of Morocco) 29
money and banking 35, 61, 80
Mongols **54–56,** 76, *84,* 116, 121, 130*c*
monotheism 12, 26, 30, 32, 66–67, 131*g*
Moorish architecture *45, 47, 48, 49,* 77
Moors 38
morality 7–8. *See also* laws
Morocco 29, 38, 47, 50, 106
mosaics 102, 107, 108, 131*g*
Moses 22, 66
mosques 51, 74, 75, 84–85, *88, 121, 132g.* *See also* specific mosque
   architecture of 49, 105–107
   depictions of humans in 24, 101
   as palaces 31
   praying and 26, 105, 106
   in the United States 14, 127, *128*
movies 13, 50, 100
Muawiya 33, 35–37, 59–60, 74, 129*c*
muezzin 105, 106
Mughals *84*
Mughira, al- *42*
Muhammad 19, 22, *23*–25, 32, 35, 93, 98, 125. *See also* Hadith; Quran
   birth and childhood 7–8, 17, 20, 50, 129*c*
   death 12, 26–27, 97, 129*c*
   depictions of *17, 23, 84,* 101
   diplomatic skills 18, 21, 23, 25, 26
   family 18, 21, 26, 27, 32, 41, 50, *52*
      marriages 17–18, 32, 33, 87
   Farewell Pilgrimage (hajj) 25–26
   followers of 20, 21, 23, 32
   Hijra 21, 30, 116
   home of 105
   Jerusalem 32
   Jews and 24
   legends and myths about 13
   Mecca 21, 25–26, 32
   Medina 21, 23, 36, 105
   messages from God 12, 18, 23, 96
   power of 21, 23
   Quran and 18, 26

Quraysh and 21, 23–24, 25
   sermons 26
   teachings 7–8, 12, 13, 18, 20–21, 22, 37, 69, 82
      slavery and 68
   warfare and 23–25, 26, 30
   writings about 20, *23,* 99
Muhammad ibn al-Qasim 40
Muharram 36
Muizz al-Dawla 46
mujahidin 125
murri naqi 81
music *42,* 89–90, 91, 92, **102–104,** *105,* 114
Muslim Brotherhood 125
Muslims 8, 13–14, 33, 53, 128. *See also* Islam; Kharijites; Sevener Shiites; Shiites; Sunnis
   conversion of 48–49, 130*c*
   non-Muslims and 12, 63, 66–68, 80, 112
   origins of 12, 20
   umma and 21, 27, 32, 59, 107, 125, 132*g*
Mutanabbi, al- 98
Mutasim, al- 63–64, 106
myrrh 10–11

N

nabidh 89
nadir 109
Nasrid sultans *45, 47, 48*
National Coffee Association 14
Nawruz 92
nay 104
nazir 109
Netherlands 40
New Testament 11
New York City 14
Niger 50
Nigeria 70
Night of Fury 31
Nile River 76
Nizam al-Mulk 89, 130*c*
nomadic life 9–10, 23–24, 83, 132*g. See also* Bedouins
Normans 51
North Africa 7, 8, 28, 38, 43, 48, 71. *See also* specific country
   Fatimid dynasty and **50–52,** 92, 129*c*
   government and politics in 45, 47
   invasions of 31, 32, 36, 129*c*
   trade and commerce in 78, 81
Nubia 76
numeral systems 118

O

oasis 11, 132*g*
Old Testament 22
olé 49
Oman 79
Omar, Mohammad 29
Omar al-Khayyam 99
On the Harmony of Religions and Philosophy (Ibn Rushd) 110
ophthalmology 113
opium 113, 114
optics 113, 119
oral tradition 96, 97, 100, 132*g*

Organization of the Islamic Conference (OIC) 122
"oriental dance" 103
Oriental rugs. *See* rugs and carpets
Osama bin Laden. *See* bin Laden, Osama
Ottoman Empire 40, 47, 71, 121, 130*c*
oud 103, 104, *105*

P

Pact of Umar 66
paintings *7*, *88*
Pakistan 8, 13, 36, 40, 70, 71, 122
palaces 31, 40, *45*, 47, *48*, 75, 107–108
Palermo 51
Palestine 10, 29, 53, 125, 127, 130*c*
Palestine Liberation Organization (PLO) 127
pancreas 109
papermaking 49, 97–98
pasta 82
pensions 63
perfume 10, 86
Persian Empire 7, 8–9, 75
    Abbasid dynasty and 61, 62, 63, 64
    culture *11*, 13, 76, 91, 95, 103
        architecture 105, 107, 108
        carpets 86
        literature 99, 100, 102, 129*c*
    government and politics 46, 62, 64
    health and medicine 111–112, 113
    invasions of 55, 121, 129*c*, 130*c*
    religion and beliefs 66
    science and technology 115, 119
    trade and commerce 10, 79, 80
Persian Gulf 10, 79
personal hygiene 83, 86, 87, 112, 115
pets 90
pharmacology 114
philosophy 95, **109–111**, 132*g*
physics **119**
pilgrimage *11*, 19, 22, 25–26, 71, 91–92, 93, 132*g*
pirates 38
Pitt, Brad 100
plaques *65*
Plato 95, 110
plays 36
Poem of Zuhair, The 97
poetry 91, **97–99**
politics. *See* government and politics
polo 91
Polo, Marco 82
polygamy 18, 87, 132*g*
polytheism 132*g*
poor 17, 20–21, 22, 67, 89
pork 83
postal system 60
pottery *11*, *12*
prayer 21, 51, *59*, 96
    call to 105, 106
    Fatimid dynasty and 51
    jinn and 13
    laws regarding 22, 71
    Mecca and 26
    mihrabs 26, 84, 106, 107, 131*g*
    rituals 19, 20, 26, 78, 92
    rugs 83, 84–85
primogeniture 45. *See also* succession
prophets 132*g*

prose **99–101**
"protectors" 63, 64, 68
protocols, royal 60, 61, 91

Q

Qaeda, al- 125, 127
qahwa, al- 14
Qanafi'l Tibb, al- (Ibn Sina) 114
qanun 103–104
qasida 98
qibla 26, 106, 132*g*
qirat 80
qitara 104
qiyas 70, 71
Quran 22, 96–97, 129*c*. *See also* laws
    afterlife and 20, 30, 92
    astronomy and 115
    banking and 80
    children and 66, 90
    class system and 20, 64–65
    death and burial 92–93
    depictions of *7*, 19, 80, 85, *95*, 101, 102
    education and 90
    jinn and 13
    Kaaba and 19
    laws and 59, **69–71**, 80
    marriage and 86–87, 89, 91
    non-Muslims and 66
    origins of 18, 20, 26, 96
    philosophy and 110
    prayer and 20, 26
    slavery and 20, 59, 68, 91
    warfare and 23, 24, 31, 32
    women and 86–87, 89, 91
quran 18
Quraysh 17, 18, 21, *23*, 32, 121
    class system and 64–65, 68
    power of 12, 25
    raids and 23–24

R

raids 23–25, 29–32, 38–40, 47, 109
raks sharki 103
Ralph of Coggeshall 55
Ramadan 22, 92
Razi 112, 115
razzia 23
record keeping 61, 74, 115
reign 132*g*
religion and beliefs 11, 22, 66–67, 101–102.
    See also Allah; God; monotheism;
    mosques; prayer; sacred texts; sharia;
    specific religion or belief
    theocracy 59, 122, 132*g*
    tolerance of 12, 45, 51, *65*, 66, 74
Renaissance, European 8
reservoirs 10, 132*g*
revolutions 9, 124, 129*c*
Richard I (king of England) 55
Ridda wars 28
"rightly guided" caliphs 27. *See also* specific
    caliph
rituals 19, 20, 26, 78, 92, 132*g*
Roger (Norman ruler) 51
Roma (Gypsy) 104
Roman Empire 8, *11*, 77
Rome 10
rosary beads 78
Rubaiyyat of Omar Khayyam (Khayyam) 99

rugs and carpets 83–*84*, 86, 91
Russia 13

S

Saad ibn Abi Waqqas 30–31, 74
sacred texts **96–97**. *See also* specific text
sadaqa 22
Safa 93
saffah, al- 41
sakk 80
Saladin (Salah al-Din) *35*, 50, 51, 54, 55, 130*c*
salat 22
Saluki 90
Samarra 64, 106, 108
samt 109
Sassanian Empire 8–9, *11*, 12, 29–32
Satan 13, 26
Saudi Arabia 7–8, 70, 125, 127. *See also*
    specific city
saum 22
sawt 103
Sayf a-Dawla 98–99
science and technology 43, 49, 81, 95–96, 109, **115–119**. *See also* health and
    medicine
Scott, Ridley 50
secularism 70, 90, 92, 101, 102, 121, 128
sekan-jabin 82
self-flagellation 36
Seljuk dynasty 46–47, 51, 53, *54*, 63, 85, 129*c*, 130*c*
September 11th 127
Sevener Shiites 56
Seville 49
sexual relations 22, 26
Shafii, Muhammad ibn Idris al- 71
Shafii law school 71
shahada 22
shahid 125. *See also* martyrs
shah mat 91
Shapur I (king of Persia) *11*
sharia 69, 70, 122, 125, 128, 132*g*
shay 118
Shiites 22, 74, **123–125**
    Abbasid dynasty and 43, 45
    government and politics 122, 124–125
    Kharijites 33, 50, 71, 78, 129*c*
    legal system 71, 122
    origins of 27, 123–124, 129*c*
    Sevener 56
    Umayyad dynasty and 36, 37, 41, 66, 129*c*
ships. *See* boats and ships
shiviti 65
shrines *73*
Sicily 40, *40*, 51
siege warfare 29–30, 132*g*
sifr 109
silk 19, 36, 61, 78, 80–81, *84*
Sinbad (movie) 100
sira 99
Siraf 79
slaves/slavery 21, 32, **68–69**, 103
    caliphs and 62, 68
    depictions of *67*
    Five Pillars of Islam and 22
    as government officials 69
    Quran and 20, 59, 68, 91
    as soldiers 52, 63–64

trade of 78
women and children 24, 68, 69, 87, 89, 91
Smith, Captain John 14
soap making 87
social class. *See* class system
Solomon 32
Somniorum Visone, De (Kindi, al-) 119
Sophocles 96
South America 14
Southeast Asia 71, 78
Soviet Union 122, 125
Spain 71, 130*c. See also* specific city
    culture 102, 109
        architecture 45, 47, 48, 49, 77
        music and 103, 104
    geography and climate 41
    government and politics 45, 47–48
    horses and 28, 41
    invasions of 38, 40, 68, 129*c*, 130*c*
    Seljuk Turks and **47–50**
    trade and commerce 49, 81, 87
    Umayyad dynasty and 43, 47, 77, 129*c*
Spanish Inquisition 48, 49, 130*c*
spices 10, 54, 81, 82
steel 36
Stone of Felicity 19
succession 132*g*
    Abbasid dynasty and 41, 45, 50, 62
    after death of Abu Bakr 29, 36
    after death of Muhammad 26–27,
        59–60, 123
    Saladin and 59
    Umayyad dynasty and 50, 107
Sudan 122
sugar 49, 51, 82, 123
sultans 46–47, 63
Sulyman 39
Sumerians 104
Summa Theologica (Thomas Aquinas) 111
sunna 59, 97, 110. *See also* Hadith
Sunnis 36, 56, **123–125**
    class system and 66
    government and politics 50, 59,
        124–125
    Hadith and 97
    law schools 707–1
    origins of 27, 37, 123–124, 129*c*
    Umayyad dynasty and 66
swirling 49
Sword of Islam. *See* Khalid ibn al-Walid
Syria 70, 74. *See also* specific city
    Crusades and 50, 53
    culture 11, 12, 95–96, 98, 102
        architecture 35, 59, 105, 107
    government and politics 43, 60, 63
    health and medicine 112
    invasions of 29–30, 33, 40, 66, 129*c*, 130*c*
    Pact of Umar 66
    trade and commerce 10, 11
    Umayyad dynasty and 60, 63

T

tabla 104
Tahir 45–46
Taif 11, 21, 29
Tajikistan 122
Taliban 29, 122, 125
taqiyya 122–123

tariffs 80
Tariq ibn Ziyad 37, 38, 41
taxation 9, 12, 22, 30
    bureaucracy and 60, 61, 62–63, 80
    class system and 65, 66, 67
taziya 36
technology. *See* science and technology
terra-cotta 12
textiles 132*g. See also* clothing
theocracy 59, 122, 132*g*
theology 111
Thomas Aquinas (saint) 51, 77, 111
Thousand and One Nights 13, 100
Three Wise Men 11
tiles, decorative 77, 85, 105, 106, 107, 108
tiraz 80–81
tithes 22
Toledo 49
tombs 35
Tours, battle of 129*c*
trade and commerce 8–9, 11, 36, 54,
    78–81, 87, 131*g*
    Baghdad as center of 75, 76
    caravans and 10, 17–18, 23, 78–79
    food 14, 49, 82
translations 99–100, 111, 129*c*
    of Greek texts 43, 51, 90, 95–96, 102,
        103, 108–109, 119
transportation 9, 76, 78, 79
tribes 7, 9–10, 11, 21, 24, 30, 46, 77. *See also*
    specific tribe
    conquering of 12, 25, 26, 27–28
    military of 38, 63, 74
    oral tradition of 87, 97
    as rulers 35, 45–46, 56, 59
troubadours 104
tunic 85, 132*g*
Tunisia 50, 121
Turkey 47, 68, 130*c*
    culture 17, 23, 54, 69, 86, 102
    government and politics 121
    laws 70–71
Turkmen 46. *See also* Seljuk dynasty
Turkmenistan 8, 122
Turks 63, 64, 68. *See also* Seljuk dynasty
Tusi, Nasir al-Din al- 116

U

Ubayd Allah 50
Uhud, battle of 25
Umar ibn Abd al-Aziz 66
Umar ibn al-Khattab 29, 30, 32, 66, 73, 74,
    116, 129*c*
Umayyad dynasty **36–42**
    class system and 64, 65, 66, 69
    culture 42, 47, 95, 103, 105–108
    Egypt and 43
    government and politics 32–33, 37-38,
        59–61
    military 35, 38–40, 60, 63
    Muawiya and 33, 35–37
    religion and beliefs 35, 59
        Shiites 36, 37, 41, 66, 129*c*
        Sunnis 66
    Spain and 43, 47, 77, 129*c*
    Syria and 60, 63
Umayyad Mosque 35, 59, 107

umma 21, 27, 32, 59, 107, 125, 132*g*
umra 19. *See also* hajj; pilgrimage
United States 14, 77, 83, 86, 124–125, 127,
    128
University of Cairo 52
University of Naples 51
upper class 20–21, 64, 83, 89, 90. *See also*
    Quraysh
Urban II (pope) 52–53
Uthman ibn Affan 32, 33, 96, 129*c*
Uzbekistan 8, 40, 55, 122

V

Valerian (emperor of Rome) 11
Visigoths 77
viziers 62, 132*g. See also* specific viziers

W

Walid, Abd al-Mulik al- 107
wallahi 49
Walt Disney Studios 13, 100
warfare 8–9, 10, 56. *See also* jihad; military;
    weaponry; specific battle, war, region
    or country
    animals and 24, 28, 29, 31, 33, 54, 74, 81
    depictions of 11, 23, 40, 54
    Quran and 23, 24, 31
    tactics and strategies 23–24, 28, 29–30,
        38, 54, 132*g*
water 9, 11, 29, 30, 114
    management of 10, 43, 76, 131*g*
    personal hygiene and 83, 86, 87
    sacredness of 82, 92, 93, 106
wazirs. See viziers
wealthy 20–21, 64, 83, 89, 90. *See also*
    Quraysh
weaponry 23, 28, 37, 38, 56, 67, 81
    battering rams 29, 30
West Africa 71
West Bank 127
Western Roman Empire 8
women 70, **86–90**, 103, 106, 127. *See also*
    harems
    as concubines 69, 91, 131*g*
    head covering 85, 87–88, 93
    Quran and 86–87, 89, 91
    slavery and 24, 68, 69, 87, 89, 91
World War II 121
writing. *See* language and writing

Y

Yathrib 11, 12, 21. *See also* Medina
Yazid I 36, 37, 99
Yazid III 69
Yemen 10, 14

Z

zakat 22
Zamzan well 92, 93
Zanj 68-69
zenith 109
zephyrum 109
zero 109, 118
Ziryab 103
Zoroaster 8
Zoroastrianism 8, 62, 65, 66

ABOUT THE AUTHOR

ROBIN DOAK, a former editor of *Weekly Reader* and *U.S. Kids* magazine, has 18 years of experience writing for children. She has written more than 35 books for young readers on various subjects including history, geography, and science.

Historical consultant STEPHEN CORY received his Ph.D. in Islamic history from the University of California at Santa Barbara in 2002. He is currently an assistant professor of history and religious studies at Cleveland State University in Cleveland, Ohio.